PEARSON
my World GEOGRAPHY

D1405207

Overview

PEARSON

Boston, Massachusetts • Chandler, Arizona • Glenview, Illinois • Upper Saddle River, New Jersey

The people who made up the *myWorld Geography* team—representing composition services; core design, digital, and multimedia production services; digital product development; editorial; editorial services; materials management; and production management—are listed below.

Courtney Alexander, Leann Davis Alspaugh, Sarah Aubry, Deanna Babikian, Paul Blankman, Alyssa Boehm, Peter Brooks, Susan Brorein, Megan Burnett, Todd Christy, Neville Cole, Bob Craton, Michael Di Maria, Glenn Diedrich, Frederick Fellows, Jorgensen Fernandez, Thomas Ferreira, Patricia Fromkin, Andrea Golden, Mary Ann Gundersen, Christopher Harris, Susan Hersch, Paul Hughes, Judie Jozokos, John Kingston, Kate Koch, Stephanie Krol, Karen Lepri, Ann-Michelle Levangie, Salena LiBritz, Courtney Markham, Constance J. McCarty, Laurie McKenna, Anne McLaughlin, Rich McMahon, Mark O'Malley, Alison Muff, Jen Paley, Gabriela Perez Fiato, Judith Pinkham, Paul Ramos, Charlene Rimsa, Marcy Rose, Rashid Ross, Alexandra Sherman, Owen Shows, Melissa Shustyk, Jewel Simmons, Ted Smykal, Emily Soltanoff, Kara Stokes, Frank Tangredi, Simon Tuchman, Elizabeth Tustian, Merle Uuesoo, Alwyn Velasquez, Andrew White, Heather Wright

Maps
XNR Productions, Inc.

Illustrations
Kerry Cashman, Marcos Chin, Dave Cockburn, Jeremy Mohler

Photography
1, (myWorld 123) **L,** Shutterstock; **R,** sinopictures/Peter Arnold; (myWorld 124) AP Images; **4,** L, Robert Harding Picture Library Ltd/Alamy; **5,** (images on map, clockwise) Robert Harding Picture Library Ltd/Alamy; Hiroji Kubota/Magnum; Kazuyoshi Nomachi/Corbis; Liu Liqun/Corbis; Nigel Hicks/Alamy; Panorama Media (Beijing) Ltd./Alamy; (images on poster) T, Indranil Mukherjee/AFP/Getty Images; M, Melanie Stetson Freeman/*The Christian Science Monitor*/Getty Images; B, PCL/Alamy; BL, AP Images; **14,** Siri Stafford/Getty Images, Inc.; **16,** Photo courtesy of Grant Wiggins; **20,** Photo courtesy of Jim Cummins; **21,** Pearson Education, Inc./Merrill; **22,** Supri Suharjoto/Shutterstock; **25,** iStockphoto.com/Royalty Free; **26,** AJSlife/Alamy; **28,** L, Dorling Kindersley; R, Shutterstock; **33,** Pearson Learning Group; **37,** Digital Vision/age Fotostock; **38–39,** Shutterstock; **41,** Merrill Education; **45,** TR, iStockphoto.com; **45,** TL, Merrill Education **45,** BL, Merrill Education; **49,** Luba V. Nel/Shutterstock; **55,** Shutterstock; **60,** Stock4b-RF/Getty Images; **61,** Shutterstock

ISBN-13: 978-0-13-369585-4
ISBN-10:   0-13-369585-9
2 3 4 5 6 7 8 9 10 V064 14 13 12 11 10

Master Teachers and Contributing Authors

George Sabato
Past President,
California Council for
the Social Studies
Placerville Union School District
Placerville, California

Michael Yell
Past President,
National Council for
the Social Studies
Hudson Middle School
Hudson, Wisconsin

Program Authors

Gregory H. Chu
Professor and Chair of Department of
Geography
University of Wisconsin-La Crosse
La Crosse, Wisconsin

Don Holtgrieve
Department of Planning, Public
Policy and Management
University of Oregon
Eugene, Oregon

Susan Hardwick
Department of Geography
University of Oregon
Eugene, Oregon

Program Consultant

Grant Wiggins
President of Authentic Education
Hopewell, New Jersey

Teacher Consultants

James F. Dowd IV
Pasadena, California

Susan M. Keane
Rochester Memorial School
Rochester, Massachusetts

Timothy T. Sprain
Lincoln Middle School
LaCrosse, Wisconsin

Marilyn Weiser
North Dakota Geographic
Alliance Coordinator
Minot State University
Minot, North Dakota

CONTENTS

ProGuide Overview

The Journey Begins With
ESSENTIAL

myWorld Geography incorporates Understanding by Design®, co-created by program author Grant Wiggins. The UbD process begins by asking an "Essential Question," with the goal of focusing on the desired understanding that students should acquire, and works backward to that understanding. Your students will be able to explore concepts, build knowledge, and transfer what they've learned beyond the classroom.

Why Essential Questions?

Each Essential Question provides a larger framework to guide students and help them see the big idea of each chapter. Woven throughout each lesson, activity, and assessment, the Essential Questions help students to

- connect to the content by activating prior knowledge and engaging them in each lesson

- experience history through meaningful hands-on activities

- transfer their knowledge to new learning situations that demonstrate true understanding

"We want students to understand . . . the goal is UNDERSTANDING, not superficial knowledge."

Grant Wiggins, *myWorld Geography* author

QUESTIONS

Hands-on Activity

EXPERIENCE

Technology Activity

CONNECT

Reading

Essential
?
Questions

UNDERSTAND

Success ✦ Tracker™

Assessment

ENDURING
UNDERSTANDING

CONNECT

Help students develop a deeper understanding of the content by making personal connections to the people and places they learn about throughout the lessons and activities.

myStory

These real-life stories are the personal accounts of teens from all over the world. Through the experiences of their international peers, your students will develop an awareness of, and relate to, different cultures and regions—right from their desks!

Destination Welcome / **Itinerary** / **Project**

/ On Assignment / Overview / Background

Language Lesson

Language Lesson

Class _____ Date _____

ct to myStory:
Xiao's Story

wo changes you have seen in your ne
se changes good or bad? Explain wh

hanges has Qian Xiano seen in his
hem in the chart under the correc

Lake Ta

do you think these changes ar
ctions.

Environmental Challenges

As the Chinese economy has grown, pollution has become a major problem. China also uses many resources to feed, clothe, and house its large population.

Facing Environmental Problems Chinese cities have some of the worst air pollution in the world. Millions of cars, buses, and coal-burning electricity plants contribute to the smog around Chinese cities.

Water pollution is also a serious problem. Factories and farms dump dangerous chemicals into rivers and lakes near cities. Lake Tai near Xiao's home is one of many lakes affected by this issue.

Drier areas in the north and west are struggling with shortages of water. Factories, farms, and citizens compete to use this limited resource. At times, the Huang River dries up before reaching the sea. The land around Beijing is so dry that sandstorms blow into the city.

China has laws to limit pollution, but local governments do not want to punish polluters too harshly. People would lose their jobs if factories closed down.

Searching for Energy In the past, China could produce all the energy it needed. Now, more energy is needed to run its many new businesses. China has started importing oil. Also, it has been building more coal-burning power plants.

Burning oil and coal makes China's air pollution even worse, so China is looking for cleaner forms of energy. In western China, wind power produces electricity. The Chinese government also built the Three Gorges Dam along the Chang River to produces **hydroelectricity** (hy droh ee lek TRIH suh tee), or electricity made by water power. Building this dam was disruptive and expensive. China's leaders have to balance these costs with the need for new sources of energy.

Reading Check What kinds of environmental challenges does China face?

Story Photo

Xiao, like many Chinese people, boils his water to make it safe to drink.

Chapter 21 Section 3

Section **3** Assessment

Key Terms
1. What is a single-party state?
2. What is illiteracy?

Key Ideas
3. **Compare and Contrast** How has reform been different in China and Mongolia?
4. **Analyze Cause and Effect** What effect does geography have on Mongolia's economic growth?

5. **Problem Solving** What is one problem that China faces? Suggest one way that China could solve this problem.

Essential Question

How can you measure success?

6. What is one way that China has been successful? Give evidence from the text and from figures to support your point. Go to your Student Journal to record your answe

Understanding by Design (UbD)

Academic research, including Understanding by Design, has informed the myWorld instructional design. Each chapter begins with an Essential Question that frames the lesson and leads students to unlock the answer through the stories, digital activities, games, student journal, and projects. When students arrive at the answer, they gain transferable knowledge.

Chapter 21

China and Its Neighbors

? Essential Question

How can you measure success?

KEY
— National border
⊕ Capital city
○ Other city

MONGOLIA

CHINA

Where in the World Are China and Its Neighbors?

n, D.C., to Wuxi: 7,440 miles

? Essential Question

How can you measure success?

guage Lesson

guage Lesson

my World IN NUMBERS

China has **10%** of the world's good farmland to feed **20%** of the world's population.

myWorld in Numbers

Help students comprehend global statistics by simplifying them into easy-to-understand explanations that they can relate to with this feature. For example, "If there were one hundred people in the world, 61 would be from Asia and 7 would be from North America."

EXPERIENCE

Take students across the globe—no passport required! With innovative online resources, project-based activities, and unprecedented customization options, all students will go beyond the printed page and actively experience the world in which they live.

On Assignment
myWorldGeography.com

On Assigment is a game-like project based on an Essential Question. Students gather information to complete the project by watching video interviews and stories, working through simulations, completing animated activities, and analyzing maps, data, artifacts, and primary sources. They capture their thoughts and record their observations in a PDA "tracker" and send their "assignment" directly to their teachers.

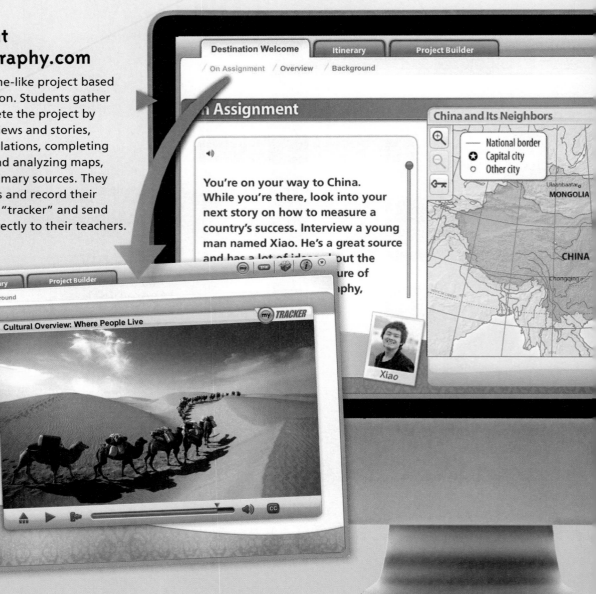

China and Its Neighbors

Essential Question
How can you measure success?

KEY
National border
Capital city
Other city

400 km
Lambert Conformal Conic Projection

MONGOLIA

Beijing

Yellow Sea

CHINA

Shanghai

East China Sea

TAIWAN

Hong Kong

South China Sea

Where in the World Are China and Its Neighbors?

Student Edition

The core components—the Student Edition, the Student Journal, the hands-on activities, and the virtual travel assignment—are tied together through UbD-based Essential Questions so they can be used in any combination, depending on teacher preference. The standards-based print textbook is supported with a host of digital and print resources that make teaching adaptable and flexible.

China and Its Neighbors: Climate

KEY
Climate
Arid
Semiarid
Tropical wet and dry
Humid subtropical
Continental, warm summer
Continental, cool summer
Subarctic
Tundra
National border
City

MONGOLIA

CHINA

Plateau of Tibet

Yellow Sea

Shanghai

East China Sea

TAIWAN

Guangzhou

Hong Kong

Hainan

South China Sea

Bay of Bengal

400 km
Lambert Conformal Conic Projection

China and Its Neighbors: Physical

KEY
Elevation
Feet | Meters
15,000 | 4,572
10,000 | 3,048
5,000 | 1,524
3,000 | 914
2,000 | 610
1,000 | 305
500 | 152
Sea level | Sea level

National border

400 km

Manchurian Plain

Taklimakan Desert

North China Plain

Plateau of Tibet

Mt. Everest

Sichuan Basin

Yellow Sea

East China Sea

South China Sea

Hainan Island

Bay of Bengal

Map Skills
Location Read the key. What do the colors on the map represent?

Place Describe how the land changes from east to west in China.

Places to Know! Label the following places on the outline map in your Student Journal: Huang River, Chang River, North China Plain, Plateau of Tibet.

Active Atlas

TRACKER

123

N

Next

2 of 2

Back

Activity-based Learning

Active learning inspires students to obtain an enduring understanding of the content they're studying and to develop confidence and self-direction as they move through both team-based and independent work. Hands-on activities are embedded in the student materials and extended through the Pro Guide Teacher's Edition, Activity Cards, Essential Question posters, and *myWorld Geography* wall maps.

Essential Questions
How much does geography shape a country?

my **World**

Carolina, from Mexico

Climate
Climate shapes the way that people live. Different patterns of temperature and precipitation can lead to very different clothing styles, housing, and ways of life.

A woman in Banga

Resources
People depend on the environment to survive. We need the environment to provide energy, food, water, and other materials. The availability of resources affects where and how people live.

A young woman uses to make a shelter in C

...ulation
...ulation is spread unevenly over the ...s surface. Some places have ... people. Other places are almost ... The distribution and density ...ple in a country have important ... on a region.

myWorld Geography **124** An Education Gap: Literacy

You are part of a research team investigating education in China. The graph at the right shows the percent of males and the percent of females who were literate. *Literate* means that a person knows how to read. Literacy rate refers to the percent of people who know how to read. For example, a literacy rate of 80 means that on average 80 out of 100 people know how to read.

Which group is more likely to be literate in China, men or women?

Literacy Rates for Men and Women

100%
80%
60%
40%
20%
0%
Women   Men

SOURCE: China Statistical Yearbook, 2007

...affect a country?

UNDERSTAND

Make sure students aren't just reading content—make sure they "get it"! In addition to the UbD approach embedded throughout the program, we provide opportunities for students to demonstrate what they've learned so you can assess for success!

Student Journal

The perfect complement for virtual world travel. This colorful, interactive student journal reinforces the Essential Question for every chapter in the program. The Student Journal provides a prereading and previewing exercise using the Essential Question. In addition to graphic organizers, chapter support in the Journal concludes with a two-page writing exercise.

China and Its Neighbors: Population Density

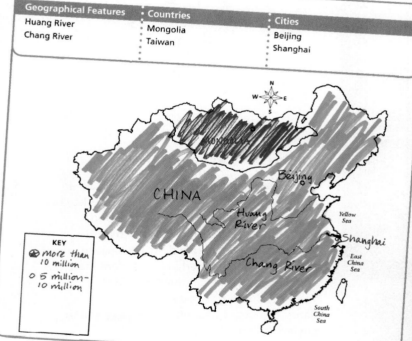

Name Adam V.

Class _____ Date _____

Take Notes

Map Skills Use the maps in your book to make a key and to label the Places to Know on the outline map below.

Places to Know!

Geographical Features	Countries	Cities
Huang River	Mongolia	Beijing
Chang River	Taiwan	Shanghai

KEY
- ⊙ more than 10 million
- ○ 5 million–10 million

MONGOLIA

CHINA

Beijing

Huang River

Yellow Sea

Shanghai

Chang River

East China Sea

South China Sea

? **Essential Question**

How can the Chinese government measure whether or not the policy has worked?

If the population stops growing or goes
then maybe the policy has been working

cities and farms are on the flatter west coast of the island. Almost three quarters of Taiwan's population lives in the coastal cities.

In contrast, Mongolia is a l[and]locked nation, or a nation without a [coast]line. About half of all Mongo[lians are] nomadic, moving their h[erds] herds of livestock acros[s the] grassy plains. The no[mads] called gers (gehrz) [...] the population li[ves in...] thi[rd] of the [...] city of U[...]

In M[...]

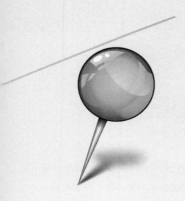

Online Project Builder

After your students have gone on their virtual journey, you can determine what knowledge they've acquired by assigning them to deliver classroom presentations or write a blog about their personalized experiences of the lessons. Students use a "tracker" PDA tool to collect the resources as part of their travel assignment. These assets—notes, pictures, audio, and video—are organized on slide templates and become a memoir of their experience.

Success ✦ Tracker™

Success Tracker is an online, formative assessment and remediation management system. Students take online assessments and are provided instant feedback on areas of weakness. Teachers receive test results and get the reporting they need to evaluate students and classes on state standards of performance.

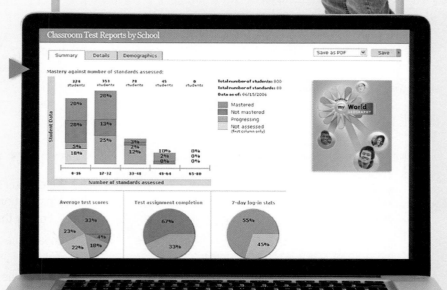

How to Use the myWorld Unit ProGuide

Pearson Education has created an exciting new way to provide instructional support to teachers. Now, for each unit, teachers will refer to a lightweight, unit-specific guide—that's right, just one book to hold at a time—with comprehensive lesson plans, an activity-based curriculum, and reproducible student resources. Review these pages to know how to get the most out of each myWorld Geography Unit Guide!

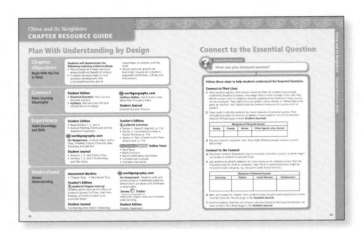

Planning the Lessons
Chapter and Core Concepts Resource Guides

Before each new chapter or Core Concepts part, there is a six-page Chapter Resource Guide or two-page Part Resource Guide to help you plan your lessons and ensure student learning. Read the Chapter or Part Resource Guide to be well prepared for what lies ahead.

Plan With Understanding by Design

myWorld Geography was written "with the end in mind," meaning each chapter was developed with a set goal for bringing about certain understandings, knowledge, and skills in the students who participate in this program. This page

- outlines how students will attain the chapter's Enduring Understandings, or big ideas.
- shows you how to assess whether students achieved understanding.
- explains how different pieces of myWorld Geography work together.

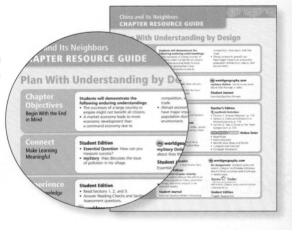

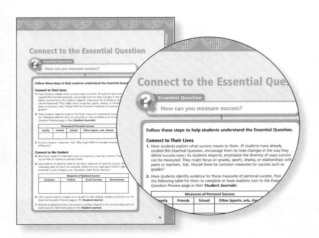

Connect to the Essential Question

Use the chapter Essential Question to guide discussions, direct instruction, and create deep, authentic learning experiences. Follow the instructions on this page to help students

- unpack the meaning of the Essential Question.
- make personal connections to the Essential Question.
- connect the Essential Question to chapter content.

Explore worldgeography.com

To get the most out of the online offerings, preview which activities are offered for each part or chapter on myworldgeography.com.

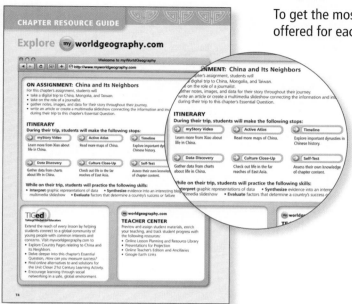

- Find descriptions of what students will do while On Assignment in the region.
- Preview the online Visual Glossary's featured terms for each Core Concepts part.
- Learn how students will use country data and online Essential Question activities.
- Find a wealth of resources to help your students to succeed with the myworldgeography.com Student and Teacher Centers.

Assess Enduring Understandings: myWorld Chapter Activity Step-by-Step Instructions and Activity Supports

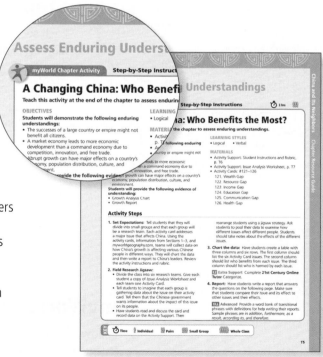

- Each chapter has a comprehensive end-of-chapter activity to assess student understanding of the chapter's Enduring Understandings.
- Step-by-Step Instructions with differentiation for diverse learners walk you through the activity.
- The first Activity Support lists student instructions and clarifies expectations with a rubric.
- The second Activity Support helps students complete the activity. Give it to them at the appropriate time as indicated in Step-by-Step Instructions.

Section Lesson Plan

Follow these instructions for teaching each section of the chapter:

- Before teaching, review the lesson's Objectives, Expectations, links to Core Concepts, and the three major steps of the lesson: Connect, Experience, and Understand.
- Use the Section Resource Guide to identify program resources that support the lesson.
- Find useful Differentiated Instruction tips throughout the lesson.
- Follow instruction in **ELL Support** to help English language learners access content and extend language skills.

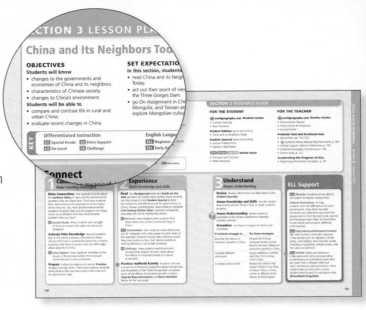

myWorld Activity Step-by-Step Instructions

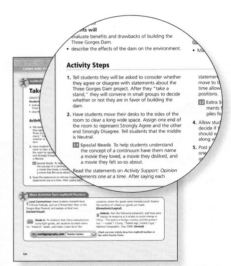

Each section has its own activity to enrich students' learning. Follow these activity steps to

- preview the objectives, materials, learning style, and groupings to prepare to teach this activity.
- engage students in a rich learning experience that reinforces section Key Ideas.
- review alternative activity choices in More Activity Ideas.

myWorld Activity Support

Follow the directions in the Step-by-Step Instructions to know when to distribute the Activity Support. Each Activity Support starts with directions for the student.

Section Quiz

Use this quiz to assess the section's Key Terms and Key Ideas.

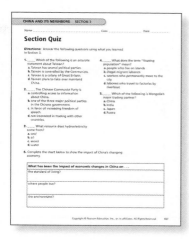

Enrichment

Use this handout to help students attain more in-depth knowledge related to the section.

Core Concepts Lesson Plan and myWorld Activity Support

Core Concepts may be taught as

- an introductory unit in your Geography course.
- individual lessons throughout the year as needed to support instruction.

Follow the steps of these abbreviated Lesson Plans and myWorld Activity Supports to

- help students acquire critical foundations for learning geography.
- conduct a myWorld Activity reinforcing the lesson's Core Concepts.

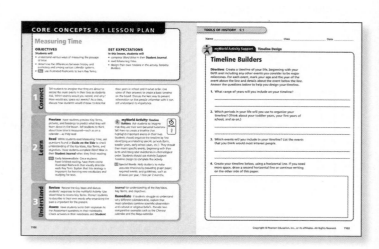

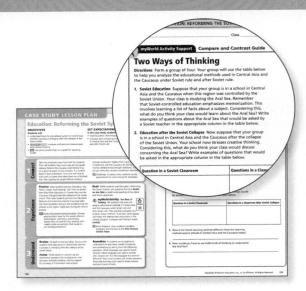

Case Study Lesson Plan and myWorld Activity Support

Follow the steps of these abbreviated Lesson Plans and myWorld Activity Supports to

- study a particular issue or aspect of a region in depth.
- conduct a myWorld Activity related to the Case Study.

Teachers using the Survey edition of myWorld Geography will find Case Study student pages online.

Primary Source Lesson Plan and myWorld Activity Support

Follow the steps of these abbreviated Lesson Plans and myWorld Activity Supports to

- help students analyze a primary source related to the chapter content.
- conduct a myWorld Activity related to understanding the primary source.

Teachers using the Survey edition of myWorld Geography will find Primary Source student pages online.

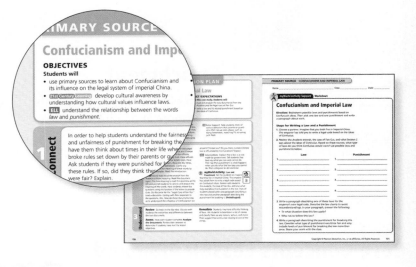

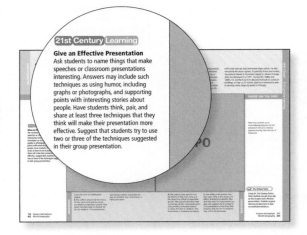

21st Century Learning Activity

Every unit ends with a 21st Century Skills challenge.

- Have students complete the activity as a class to practice the skill.
- Then have students use the 21st Century Online Tutor to further explore this skill.
- Find online alternatives to and solutions for the Unit Closer 21st Century Learning Activity.

Teaching the Lessons
Preview

At the beginning of each Regional Overview, myStory, and section, you will find Preview instructions above the student page to help students to

- activate prior knowledge.
- build background.
- prepare to learn.

Guide on the Side

To the right and left sides of all student pages, you will find point-of-use questions and references to enrich your lesson. Use Guide on the Side to

- model active reading and metacognitive thinking.
- encourage critical thinking by asking lower- to higher-order questions.
- help students analyze maps, charts, and other visuals.
- know when to direct students to myworldgeography.com, 21st Century Online Tutor, the Student Journal, or a myWorld Activity.

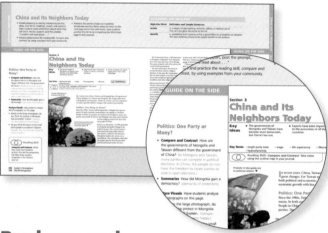

Background

At the top of most student pages you will find Background notes. Prepare to teach by reading these notes, primary sources, and other facts. Use information to

- hook students' interest.
- build students' background knowledge and vocabulary.
- enliven a discussion.
- make connections to other skills and content.
- prevent misunderstandings.
- advance your own knowledge of the content area.

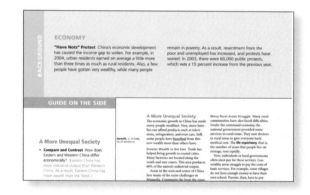

Answers

- At the bottom of most student pages, you will find answers to Reading Checks, Chart Skills, Map Skills, and the Section Assessment. Answers to the Chapter Assessment appear in all the margins of the Chapter Assessment pages.

Professional Development:
Growing as a Teacher Through myWorld

MyWorld Geography is a comprehensive middle grades social studies program designed to engage and meet the needs of all students. At Pearson, we are committed to supporting you as a professional, an academic, and an educator. Through the textbook, online resources, activities, and other resources, *myWorld Geography* has implemented the finest teaching practices used in the classrooms across the United States. From backward planning to differentiated instruction to 21st century skills, the myWorld program and the myWorld ProGuide are links between your classroom and the cutting edge of educational research.

The best way to learn about the pedagogy found in *myWorld Geography* is to read the articles that address the different philosophies and strategies found in this program. On the following pages, you will find articles on these topics:

- Understanding by Design
- Teaching English language learners
- Technology in the classroom
- 21st century learning environments
- Reading in the social studies classroom
- Differentiated instruction
- Learning with activities
- Grouping practices
- Assessment

Each of these articles provides
- Essential background knowledge about the theory and research behind the teaching practices our program supports
- A view into what these practices look like in the classroom
- A quick way to know where these practices show up in myWorld

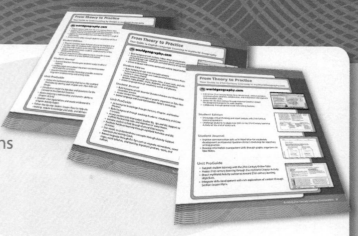

Every article ends with a section called, "From Theory to Practice," because we know what matters most is what happens after the bell sounds, with real kids, during a real myWorld lesson.

These articles will help you successfully meet the learning needs of all your students. We understand that as an educator you need to continually add to your teaching repertoire—always learning more about new theories and philosophies, new technologies, and the unique ways a new generation learns. Exploring these professional development articles is one of many ways that you can continue to grow as a teacher.

How can reading an article change your teaching? These articles are not an end in themselves, but they provide an opportunity for deeper, reflective teaching.

- Plan discussion groups around the articles or the topics.
- Keep a teaching journal or blog focused on the topic that is most essential for your students.
- Develop an online discussion board for teachers at your school to respond to the articles and how they relate to instruction at your school.

Pearson also offers ways to extend your professional development. In addition to having a Pearson trainer show teachers how to use the myWorld program, your school can invite a Pearson trainer to present a workshop on a variety of professional development topics. There are also myWorld Teacher podcasts to help you better utilize the program in your classroom.

All together, there are many levels of Pearson professional development to explore: in print, on the Web, and in person. The ProGuide professional development articles that you are about read are your entryway into successful social studies instruction.

Understanding by Design

by Grant Wiggins,
co-author of *Understanding by Design*

Grant Wiggins is the president of Authentic Education. He earned his Ed.D. from Harvard University and his B.A. from St. John's College. Dr. Wiggins consults with schools, districts, and state and national education departments on a variety of reform matters; organizes workshops; and develops resources on curricular change. He is also the coauthor, with Jay McTighe, of *Understanding by Design* and *The Understanding by Design Handbook*, the award-winning materials on curriculum published by the Association for Supervision and Curriculum Development (ASCD).

What is Understanding by Design? Understanding by Design (UbD) is a disciplined way of thinking about the design of curriculum, instruction, and assessment. The goal is for students to achieve a deep understanding of important ideas you need to teach. At the core of the UbD framework is the intention for students to break through and get it, not just for the test, but for life.

UbD provides a way to move from simply covering the curriculum to ensuring student understanding. The work of learning provides students with the opportunity to explore, test, verify, apply important concepts, and to make sense of the content.

Key Components of UbD

Key components of UbD are Backward Design, Big Ideas, Essential Questions, and Transfer.

Begin with Backward Design UbD emphasizes the use of a backward design process to develop instruction. Rather than beginning the planning process with activities, materials, or textbook content, backward design starts by identifying the desired long-term results and appropriate assessment evidence.

Three principle stages provide a conceptual framework for helping teachers design learning mindful of the big ideas of content. (See figure below.)

Plan experiences and instruction

Determine acceptable evidence

Identify desired result of instruction

Big Ideas, Big Questions In the UbD framework, big ideas give context and meaning to discrete facts and skills. What is a "big idea"? It is a powerful concept, theme, or issue that a student uses to make sense of otherwise disconnected content elements. Because big ideas are familiar and compelling, students readily connect their previous learning experiences to the new one.

Big ideas allow all students to participate in the learning, because everyone can share their ideas, values, and opinions and connect to content. Learning is thus about examining and informing students' various points of view—leading to new understanding.

One way of focusing in on a big idea is to use Essential Questions. Essential Questions are designed to challenge preconceived notions and force students to stretch their thinking, using course content to support and inform answers. In doing so, students discover meaning in the content and connections to their own lives. UbD's use of big ideas and Essential Questions encourages students to not just know something but understand why it matters and how it can be applied.

Transfer Knowledge and Skills The ultimate goal of education is to help students apply or "transfer" what they learn to new and unfamiliar situations. In the UbD framework, transfer is about students being able to stretch the limits, use creativity, and tackle realistic challenges related to core content. Transfer ability means that students can adapt their learning to fit many different settings, issues, and problems—a key aim of schooling. The ability to transfer learning also helps students to succeed with state testing: Students often fail to apply prior learning to new readings, problems, or prompts on the test. When students show that they can transfer knowledge, skills, and understandings, it means they understand the connection between the classroom and the real world. It also means students are more prepared for the real work of the disciplines they study—whether as physicians, journalists, engineers, or artists.

> *"Build your unit around one idea with power, an idea that helps learners make sense of otherwise isolated content."*
> —*Grant Wiggins*

The Essential Question
- Connects prior learning
- Promotes inquiry
- Allows for transfer
- Stimulates rethinking
- Fosters deep understanding
- Provokes lively debate

Goals for the Learning Experience

To achieve content mastery, deep understanding, and transfer, curriculum design must take into account the following goals:

- Engage students in inquiry and application
- Promote the transfer of learning
- Provide a conceptual framework to help students make sense of discrete facts and skills
- Uncover and use the big ideas of the content
- Develop appropriate assessment methods to determine the degree of student understanding, knowledge, and skills
- Address misunderstandings or biases that interfere with learning
- Fold content standards and school mission into the design work

Achieving these goals requires backward planning, starting with the goals and working backward to what the students and you will actually do. Backward curriculum design lends purpose and conviction to every lesson, every activity, and every assignment.

Stage 1
Identify what students should know, understand, and be able to do.

- Long-term transfer goals
- Key Ideas framed as understandings
- National and state content standards
- Essential Questions
- Specific knowledge and skills

Stage 2
Determine needed evidence for the knowledge, skills, and understandings identified in Stage 1.

- Authentic performance tasks
- Other assessments, labeled by which knowledge, skills, or transfer goals they assess
- Rubrics for each task, focusing on the most important unit goals

Stage 3
Plan learning experiences and instruction.

- Assess students' prior knowledge and skill levels
- Plan activities to ensure a balance of knowledge and skill acquisition, meaning making, and transfer
- Use ongoing assessments to check for understanding and make adjustments

From Theory to Practice

Your Guide to Understanding by Design in myWorld Geography

my worldgeography.com

- Acquire relevant skills with the 21st Century Online Tutor.
- Acquire and practice knowledge with Data Discovery, Active Atlas, Culture Close-up and other On Assignment features.
- Explore the Essential Question and make meaning through the myStory Video online.
- Assess transfer ability through students' completion of On Assignment.

Student Edition

- Essential Questions open dialogue around the big idea of each chapter.
- myStory helps the students make meaning of the chapter content.
- Key Ideas help students know what they need to learn.
- Section Assessment checks students' understanding of Key Ideas and the Essential Question.
- Chapter Assessment offers opportunity to transfer knowledge and skills from each section to a new format and context.

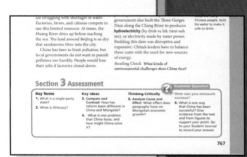

Student Journal

- Essential Question Preview gets students ready to delve deep into meaning.
- myStory pages bring about important connections between the real world and the curriculum.
- Essential Question Writers Workshop provides assessment of student long-term understanding and writing skills.

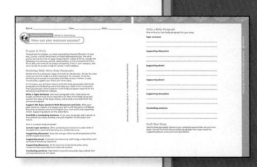

Unit ProGuide

- Follow the backward planning that led to the myWorld Geography ProGuides by starting each chapter with Plan With Understanding by Design.
- Introduce or revisit the big ideas and questions for the chapter with Connect to the Essential Question.
- Assess enduring understanding and transfer ability with the myWorld Chapter Activity.
- Establish clear expectations and assess understanding with the myWorld Chapter Activity Rubric.
- Follow step-by-step Section Lesson Plans to help students make meaning, acquire knowledge and skills, and demonstrate understanding.

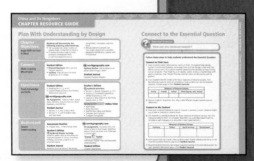

The Three Pillars of English Language Learning

by Dr. Jim Cummins,
the University of Toronto

Dr. Cummins teaches in the Department of Curriculum, Teaching, and Learning of the Ontario Institute for Studies in Education at the University of Toronto. His research has focused on the education of bilingual students and the possibilities and pitfalls of technology in education. Dr. Cummins has written and presented many works on second-language learning and literacy development, including "Language and the Human Spirit" (TESOL Matters 13, December 2002–Feb 2003) and *The International Handbook of English Language Teaching* (Springer, 2007), co-edited with Chris Davison.

Teaching social studies is as much about teaching new ideas and skills as it is about teaching language—new vocabulary, new terms, and new text structures abound in each year of social studies learning. Yet more teachers than ever before are working with students whose first language is not English. Students enter today's classrooms from diverse backgrounds, and educators are sometimes overwhelmed by the challenge of meeting every student's needs.

Teachers of students who are English language learners will find that best teaching practices for those students are often the same as best teaching practices for all students. However, there are critical understandings that a teacher must possess, about language proficiency and about the foundations of teaching language, in order to successfully support English language learners on their journey through *myWorld Geography.*

Understanding Language Proficiency

In order to understand how English learners develop second-language literacy and reading comprehension, we must distinguish among three different aspects of language proficiency.

Conversational fluency This dimension of proficiency represents the ability to carry on a conversation in face-to-face situations. Most native speakers of English have developed conversational fluency by age 5. This fluency involves the use of high-frequency words and simple grammatical constructions. English learners generally develop fluency in conversational English within a year or two of intensive exposure to the language in school or in their neighborhood environments.

Discrete language skills These skills reflect specific phonological, literacy, and grammatical knowledge that students can acquire in two ways—through direct instruction or through immersion in a literacy-rich and language-rich environment in home or in school. The discrete language skills acquired early include

- knowledge of the letters of the alphabet
- knowledge of the sounds represented by individual letters and combinations of letters
- the ability to decode written words

Children can learn these specific language skills concurrently with their development of basic English vocabulary and conversational fluency.

Academic language proficiency This dimension of proficiency includes knowledge of the less-frequent vocabulary of English as well as the ability to interpret and produce increasingly complex written language. As students progress through the grades, they encounter

- far more low-frequency words, primarily from Greek and Latin sources
- complex syntax (for example, sentences in passive voice)
- abstract expressions

Acquiring academic language is challenging. Schools spend at least 12 years trying to teach all students the complex language associated with academic success.

It is hardly surprising that research has repeatedly shown that English language learners, on average, require *at least* 5 years of exposure to academic English to catch up to native-speaker norms.

Effective instruction for English language learners is built on three fundamental pillars.

Activate Prior Knowledge and Build Background

No learner is a blank slate. Each person's prior experience provides the foundation for interpreting new information. In reading, we construct meaning by bringing our prior knowledge of language and of the world to the text. The more we already know about the topic in the text, the more of the text we can understand. Our prior knowledge enables us to make inferences about the meaning of words and expressions that we may not have come across before.

Furthermore, the more of the text we understand, the more new knowledge we can acquire. This expands our knowledge base (what cognitive psychologists call *schemata*, or underlying patterns of concepts). Such comprehension, in turn,

enables us to understand even more concepts and vocabulary.

It is more important to *activate* students' prior knowledge because students may not realize what they know about a particular topic or issue. Their knowledge may not facilitate learning unless that knowledge is brought to consciousness. Teachers can use a variety of strategies to activate students' prior knowledge:

- Brainstorming
- Discussion
- Direct experience
- Dramatization
- Visual stimuli
- Student writing
- Drawing

When students don't already have knowledge about a topic, it is important to help them acquire that knowledge. For example, in order to comprehend text such as "The Midnight Ride of Paul Revere," students need to have background in United States history.

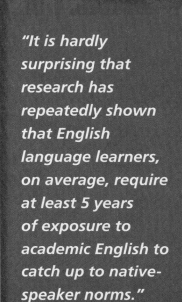

"It is hardly surprising that research has repeatedly shown that English language learners, on average, require at least 5 years of exposure to academic English to catch up to native-speaker norms."

Successful Instruction for English Language Learners

Activate Prior Knowledge — **Build Background**

Access Content

Extend Language

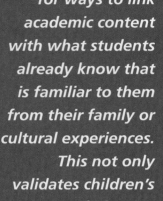

> *"We should constantly search for ways to link academic content with what students already know that is familiar to them from their family or cultural experiences. This not only validates children's sense of identity, but it also makes the learning more meaningful."*

Access Content

How can teachers make complex academic English comprehensible for students who are still in the process of learning English?

We can *scaffold* students' learning by modifying the input itself. Here are a variety of ways of modifying the presentation of the academic content to students so that they can more effectively gain access to the meaning.

Using visuals Visuals enable students to "see" the basic concepts we are trying to teach much more effectively than if we rely only on words. Among the visuals we can use are

- pictures, diagrams, and maps
- real objects
- vocabulary cards
- graphic organizers

Dramatization and acting out For beginning English learners, *Total Physical Response*, in which they follow commands such as "Turn around," can be highly effective. The meanings of words can be demonstrated through *gestures* and *pantomime*.

Language clarification This category of teaching methods includes language-oriented activities that clarify the meaning of new words and concepts. *Use of dictionaries*, either bilingual or English-only, is still the most direct method of getting access to meaning.

Making personal and cultural connections We should constantly search for ways to link academic content with what students already know and what is familiar to them from their family or cultural experiences. This not only validates children's sense of identity, but it also makes the learning more meaningful.

Extend Language

A systematic exploration of language is essential if students are to develop a curiosity about language and deepen their understanding of how words work. Students should become *language detectives* who investigate the mysteries of language and how it has been used throughout history to shape and change society.

When students know rules or conventions of how words are formed, it gives them an edge in extending vocabulary. It helps them figure out the meaning of words and how to form different parts of speech from words. The exploration of language can focus on meaning, form, or use.

Focus on meaning Categories that can be explored within a focus on meaning include

- native language equivalents or cognates
- synonyms, antonyms, and homonyms
- meaning of prefixes, roots, or suffixes

Focus on form Categories that can be explored within a focus on form include

- word families
- words with the same prefixes, roots, or suffixes
- grammatical patterns

Focus on use Categories that can be explored within a focus on use include

- general uses
- metaphorical use
- advertisements
- idioms
- proverbs
- puns and jokes

The Three Pillars

Establish a solid structure for the effective instruction of English language learners with the Three Pillars of English Language Learning:

- Activate Prior Knowledge and Build Background
- Access Content
- Extend Language

From Theory to Practice

Your Guide to English Language Learning in myWorld Geography

my worldgeography.com

- Build background with myStory Videos about young people.
- Access content with engaging, interactive visuals and sound, and clarify language with visual and animated glossary of key terms with Spanish translations.
- Extend language with online games and writing opportunities.

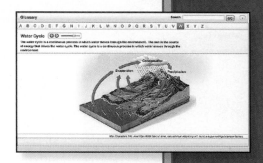

Student Edition

- Build background with Core Concepts Lessons.
- Activate prior knowledge and make personal connections through myStory in every chapter.
- Access content through the Chapter Atlas, Closer Look, and other dynamic maps, photos, charts, diagrams, and illustrations.
- Extend language through vocabulary words and glossary.

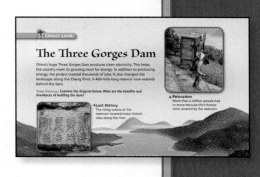

Student Journal

- Build background with Essential Question Preview and Word Wise vocabulary practice.
- Access content through conceptual graphic organizers in Take Notes.
- Extend language with Essential Question Writer's Workshop.

Unit ProGuide

- Activate prior knowledge through the Unit, Chapter, and Section Previews.
- Build background through teaching Academic Vocabulary and Core Concepts.
- Access content with blue-coded, leveled ELL tips and ELL Support to scaffold the learning steps and objectives of every lesson.
- Validate student culture through Cultural Connections.
- Facilitate hands-on learning through myWorld Activities and ELL Activities.
- Use visuals to understand new concepts through Activity Support handouts and Activity Cards.
- Extend language through ELL Tips such as cognate connections, word maps, word splashes, and teaching important prefixes, roots, and suffixes.

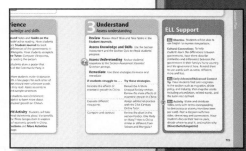

The What and Where of Technology in Your Classroom

Technology integration is about learning. It is about helping students use data and information to think critically, be creative, solve problems, and communicate. It is doing things that would otherwise be impossible or doing them better and quicker. Technology also helps us collaborate with people all over the world to accomplish these tasks. To do this successfully, we need to move from automating—putting the technology on top of what we already do—to informating. That is, we need to use technology to do things that we wouldn't otherwise be able to do. Informating will lead to digital experiences that empower students.

Automating—putting technology on top of what we already do

Informating—using technology to do things that we wouldn't otherwise be able to do

A Wellspring of Digital Resources

What does educational technology version 2.0 look like? The variety and depth of resources available to teachers has grown dramatically. Educators now have access to technology resources that allow them to

- use the Web for accessing and sharing information (blogs, wikis, TeacherTube)
- get data instantaneously (student responders, student information systems)
- learn online and move student learning online (learning management systems)
- share digital resources (interactive whiteboards and slates)
- personalize learning (laptops and artificial intelligence)

These new resources sound like they should bring us closer to reaching our goal of technology as a tool to support learning. However, the expanding utility of technology alone will not be enough to reach our goals. Fully realizing the learning potential of technology in the classroom depends upon a shift of control from the teacher to the students.

Technology-Centered Means Student-Centered

As most educators already know, in order to bring about success for all students, students must take ownership of their learning environment. In a technology-centered classroom, the teacher doesn't always have to know how to use a Web 2.0 tool, but the teacher must know the right questions to ask so that students get the most out of the tool. The goal is to empower students so that they can apply what they are learning in authentic situations. This shift of control will lead to a more student-centered environment. In a world of education that demands higher levels of personalization and differentiation, such a shift is one of the biggest benefits of digital learning.

Shifting to Digital

technology resources

Teacher-centered environment → **Student ownership of learning**

Students go on the Internet not only because they want to find information or use information, but also because they want to contribute. How do we bring that type of intrinsic motivation and participation to the classroom?

The Next Digital Generation

The PopTropica® Web site is an excellent example of how the next generation of students will be using the Web. This Web site was developed so students ages six to fifteen would be immersed in a virtual world that asks them to travel, compete head-to-head, communicate, explore, and even read books. Students participate in these kinds of online games and learning experiences because they enjoy it! They like the challenges offered by the site and the social environment.

A site like PopTropica exemplifies the fact that young Web users view the Internet differently from older users. For young users, the Web has always been a game or experience in which they could actively participate. They go on the Internet not only because they want to find information or use information, but also because they want to contribute. So the question now becomes, how do we bring that type of intrinsic motivation and participation to the classroom?

Motivating Students Through Web Tools

Countless teachers have used Web 2.0 tools in the classroom to motivate students to have powerful learning experiences. They have used these social tools to create classroom environments that have made technology ubiquitous.

One example of using Web 2.0 tools to build an engaging learning experience is from a middle school in North Carolina. The teacher developed a technology-infused project called Carbon Fighters. A class wiki explained expected outcomes, defined project roles, provided links to outside online resources, and tracked students' progress and participation.

In the introduction to the wiki, students described the problem of North Carolina's growing population, growing energy needs, and the impact of this growth on their state's environment. They then used the site to carry out a letter-writing campaign encouraging the governor to address this problem.

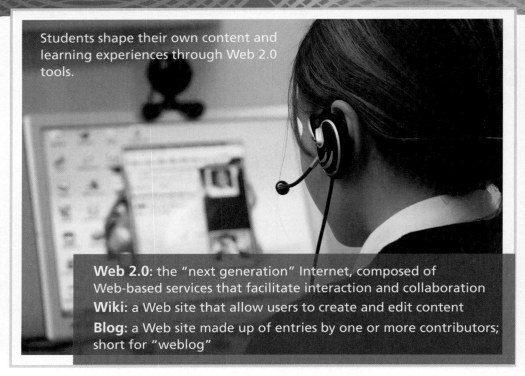

Students shape their own content and learning experiences through Web 2.0 tools.

Web 2.0: the "next generation" Internet, composed of Web-based services that facilitate interaction and collaboration
Wiki: a Web site that allow users to create and edit content
Blog: a Web site made up of entries by one or more contributors; short for "weblog"

Students used online research tools and a collaborative online writing process to produce, revise, and present their letters. Using the wiki history feature, the teacher was able to track student contributions. Students were also able to use an online rubric to assess their own work.

Another example of innovative use of Web 2.0 tools happened in an elementary classroom when the teacher set up a blog about a book the students were reading. Students used the blog to answer comprehension questions. To add excitement to the discussion, the teacher asked the author to respond to what the students wrote. With an authentic audience for students' ideas, they were more motivated to respond. The result was a detailed, rich discussion of the book.

Next Steps for Technology Integration

So what does all this mean? Technology integration happens in a student-centered classroom where learning is the most important goal. We must focus on the learning and let the technology provide opportunities to improve the learning. When control is shifted to the students and teachers begin to research and learn with the students and ask the right questions, we will begin to see a major change in education.

The Partnership for 21st Century Skills and the International Society for Technology in Education have been excellent catalysts for technology supporting the learning environment. The resources and tools available for teachers are amazing and—with high-quality professional development—can help transform the learning environment.

Research is clear that the most important piece of the change process is the classroom teacher. So start asking questions about and with technology, start sharing the great things you are doing in your classroom, and allow students to have some control over their learning. You can ensure that your students are ready for the 21st century and the digital innovations we have yet to see.

From Theory to Practice

Your Guide to Technology in myWorld Geography

my worldgeography.com

- Encourage meaningful connections through the myStory Videos online.
- Send students On Assignment as virtual traveling journalists.
- Reinforce vocabulary acquisition with the online Visual Glossary.
- Motivate students to interact with maps, graphs, and other visuals by using their Digital Trackers.
- Personalize learning with the engaging and interactive 21st Century Online Tutor.
- Have students take control of their learning with online Self-Tests.
- Assess and track progress with Success Tracker.
- Use the Online Lesson Planner to plan the instruction of each chapter or section.
- Monitor deep understanding through students' Essential Question online articles.

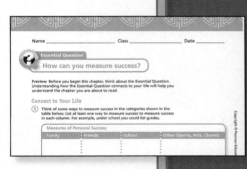

Student Edition

- Access content in the Student Edition Online with Audio.
- Draw connections between the myStory in print and the myStory Video online.
- Find myworldgeography.com to tell students when to go online.

Student Journal

- Have students access the Student Journal online to easily manage homework materials.

Unit ProGuide

- Follow myworldgeography.com buttons to know when to direct students to online maps, data, or other activities.
- Integrate the 21st Century Online Tutor into specific lesson plans and chapters.
- Access a preview of the online On Assignment journey for each chapter.
- Find directions to the online Lesson Planner and other Teacher Center resources.

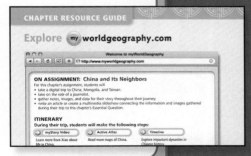

Building 21st Century Learning Environments

A high school teacher leads a fishbowl activity in which students discuss alternative fuel options. A group at the center is well versed on the pros and cons of each option. As the discussion begins, students in an outer group turn on computers and join a chat about the topic. They integrate information from both the live discussion and the Internet to enrich their chat. At the end of the lesson, the teacher asks students what they did and didn't like about the activity; a spirited debate ensues. This 21st century teacher creates an integrated learning environment, allowing digital natives to use tools with which they are familiar to evaluate and create new information. Does this sound like your school?

In December 2006, *Time* published an article titled "How to Bring Our Schools Out of the 20th Century," which concluded that schools have not changed much in the last 100 years. The author argued, "Today's economy demands not only a high-level competence in the traditional academic disciplines, but also what might be called 21st century skills." What exactly are 21st century skills and how can educators ensure students are learning in 21st century environments?

The Partnership for 21st Century Schools (P21) has developed a unified vision for 21st century learning, as expressed in the graphic on the next page. Many school districts adopted this framework and have started integrating these skills into identified outcomes for student learning.

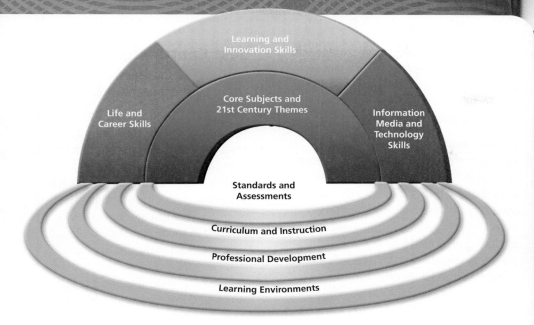

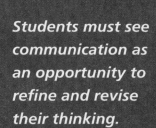

Understanding 21st Century Learning

Many educators require guidance translating the P21 vision, framework, and skills into classroom practice. As educators create 21st century learning environments, they must consider skills such as communication, collaboration, creation, information management and evaluation, as well as ethics and societal issues. These skills are not focused on technology, though it is a critical resource.

21st century creation skills Students must recognize that the ability to develop novel ideas after a careful process of synthesis and evaluation—and to edit and publish those ideas to wide audiences— is far more important than simply consuming knowledge.

Tomorrow's students must also be able to fluidly move between creative formats. While text remains the primary vehicle for expressing thoughts, students must be comfortable with a range of multimedia products that are becoming common. Finally, students must embrace the idea that work can be continually developed and revised by teams over time.

Communication skills 21st century students must be skilled communicators. Work is now driven by human interaction; the most successful members of any organization can leverage relationships to access information and to drive change.

Students must see communication as an opportunity to refine and revise their thinking. They must engage in both collaborative and competitive dialogue. They must understand different roles in complex networks of learners, respect multiple viewpoints, recognize that listening leads to productive conversations, and articulate a range of positions clearly.

Collaboration skills Digital tools have removed time and place as barriers to "teaming," so 21st century students must be skilled collaborators. Employers can now pair talented individuals—regardless of location—and expect employees to contribute to shared projects. To prepare for this, students need experience collaborating across classrooms, schools, and communities. They must be equal partners in the creation of shared documents and presentations—and have ample opportunities to create collective

Students must see communication as an opportunity to refine and revise their thinking.

final products. Collaborative experiences help students learn task management skills that are prerequisites for successful participation in a work world driven by joint endeavors.

Information management and evaluation skills Perhaps the greatest challenge facing students sifting through content is to select what is truly useful. Students of an earlier generation had access to a handful of sources while exploring new ideas; today's students have access to thousands of sources.

Students must be effective managers and evaluators of information. They must quickly access content of value to their work and be able to judge the reliability of the sources that they have chosen to use. Students must synthesize information from a variety of primary and secondary sources to make predictions, validate information, and draw verifiable conclusions. Without information literacy, students will be ineffective information users.

Ethics and Societal Issues With a few mouse clicks, today's students may stumble upon inappropriate content or participate in potentially unsafe interactions. Students must learn to guard themselves and their identities while working in virtual environments. They must recognize and have an action plan for removing themselves from dangerous situations. Age-appropriate guidance, monitoring, and guidelines will assist students as they learn to take responsibility for their own behavior when using online resources.

Copyright infringement and plagiarism issues also arise in 21st century learning environments. Students and staff must understand and follow fair use guidelines when creating multimedia presentations, making copies, using student work, and downloading files. Students and teachers must appropriately cite information to give credit to authors in a standardized way.

> *Students of an earlier generation had access to a handful of sources while exploring new ideas; today's students have access to thousands of sources.*

21st Century Instruction

Use these strategies to bring 21st century instruction into your classroom.

Project-based learning Students who take ownership of their learning are more engaged and motivated than students with little control over their studies. Project-based learning allows teachers and students to develop standards-based units of study in which students show content mastery in meaningful ways. Educators evaluate mastery based on application of student learning to various authentic tasks. The project spans the unit of study and students demonstrate mastery by creating a product over the course of the project.

21st century assessment Some teachers are disinclined to design lessons emphasizing 21st century skills because they don't see these skills having a positive effect on standardized test scores. Testing ensures a measure of uniformity between the intended and implemented curriculum, but it can also control instruction.

Organizations are conducting research on 21st century assessments. Dr. Richard Hersh proposes that teachers redirect assessment toward feedback students can use to further their learning. He also favors assessments that involve simulation and guided practice with an emphasis on authentic applications and performance to demonstrate what students know.

Sound practices supported by the right tools Perhaps most important, 21st century learning must be focused on the development of deep understanding and the long-lasting acquisition of skills, rather than teaching how to use individual digital tools. Digital tools embraced today may be gone or antiquated by tomorrow. Instead, students should see tools within the context of individual skills—facilitating creation, collaboration, communication, and information management—and become adept at transferring skills from one context to another.

From Theory to Practice

Your Guide to 21st Century Learning in myWorld Geography

my worldgeography.com

- Link to the 21st Century Online Tutor for personal, online tutorials in communication, creation, collaboration, and information management and evaluation skills.
- Assess for the 21st century through Essential Question–based On Assignment projects for each chapter.
- Collaborate through global social networking features.

Student Edition

- Encourage critical thinking and visual analysis with 21st Century Learning questions.
- Challenge students to apply new skills in the 21st Century Learning Activity at the end of every unit.

Student Journal

- Improve communication skills with Word Wise for vocabulary development and Essential Question Writer's Workshop for expository writing practice.
- Develop information management skills through graphic organizers on Take Notes.

Unit ProGuide

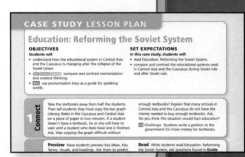

- Support student learning with the 21st Century Online Tutor.
- Assess 21st century learning through the myWorld Chapter Activity.
- Direct myWorld Activity outcomes toward 21st century learning objectives.
- Integrate skills development with rich explorations of content through Section Lesson Plans.

Reading in the Social Studies Classroom

Despite a widespread belief that students have mastered reading in the elementary grades, many middle school students still struggle with reading competence.

Social studies as a discipline is intimately connected to the use of literacy skills. In the middle school social studies classroom, a large portion of the information students are expected to learn comes from reading textbooks. Lengthy passages may be filled with unfamiliar schema and abstract concepts, expository text structures, specialized vocabulary, and various visual aids such as highlighted words, graphs, timelines, photos, and maps. Despite a widespread belief that students have mastered reading in the elementary grades, many middle school students still struggle with reading competence. Moreover, basic literacy skills are not sufficient when texts become more difficult and complex. Thus the challenge for teachers is to build not only their students' reading skills, but also their interest in more complicated types of reading materials. Explicit instruction in comprehension strategies and content-specific vocabulary within the context of social studies texts is necessary to help middle school students develop competence in critical literacy skills.

Teacher Reflection

What are some of the challenges your students face when reading and comprehending social studies text?

How can the learning of metacognitive strategies create more confident and independent readers?

Metacognition for Social Studies Reading

Learning metacognitive strategies can provide students with greater confidence and independence as readers in social studies. The goal is for metacognitive readers to be aware of what they understand, to know when their comprehension breaks down, and to apply specific strategies when they don't understand.

Comprehension strategies Teaching specific strategies can enhance students' comprehension of the social studies textbook. These strategies include pre-reading activities, such as activating relevant prior knowledge, previewing

Recognizes breakdown in comprehension	→	Applies specific reading strategies	→	Result: understanding

vocabulary, and surveying the text for clues about themes and main ideas. Helping students make personal connections supports comprehension by connecting what the reader already knows about a given topic with the new information offered in the text. Furthermore, previewing text for main ideas and concepts enables students to determine what they already know and what they will learn.

While reading, metacognitive readers apply strategies to identify the most important ideas and use a variety of strategies to achieve comprehension when it eludes them. For example, they may use graphic and semantic organizers such as concept maps and outlines. These visual structures are powerful comprehension tools because they offer concrete representations of abstract thinking processes.

Recognizing text structure Teaching readers to recognize common academic and expository text structures can also improve their overall reading comprehension. Social studies textbooks are often organized according to chronological sequence, compare and contrast, concept and definition, description, or cause and effect.

Awareness of text structure also includes analyzing the physical presentation of a text, including text features and text divisions. Text features in a typical textbook include headings, subheadings, highlighted main ideas, signal words, graphics, and captions. Additionally, the text is divided into chapters, sections, and paragraphs.

Text-mapping, a graphic technique that emphasizes the prereading process, is one strategy that facilitates an in-depth look at the structure and features of a text. Students who can map or diagram a text's organization can read a text with specific questions in mind and better understand the author's message.

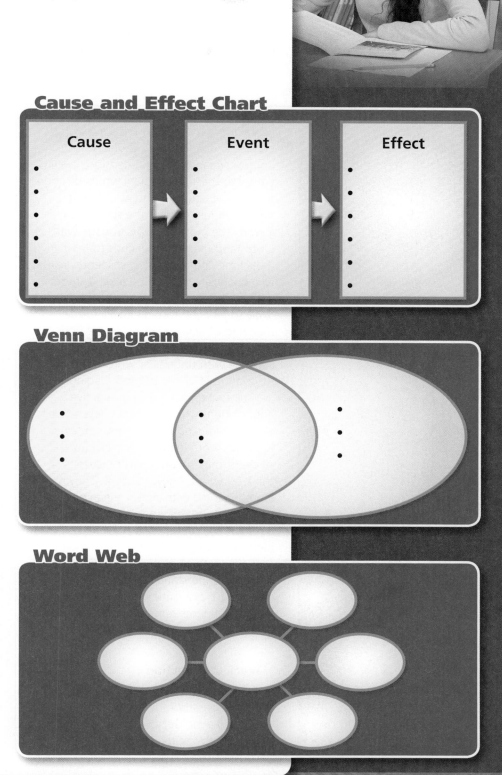

Cause and Effect Chart

| Cause | Event | Effect |

Venn Diagram

Word Web

Building Vocabulary

Academic success also requires direct instruction in content-specific vocabulary. Students need a rich body of word knowledge to succeed in basic skill areas, but they also need a specialized vocabulary to learn from the social studies textbook and in the classroom.

Given the relative difficulty of social studies texts, teaching vocabulary is very important. Teaching specific words before reading builds vocabulary and improves reading comprehension. It is critical to teach vocabulary words through a variety of activities and at different times, not just once at the start of the lesson. The more students engage with words and make connections to their meanings, the more likely students are to recognize words in the text. A student with a bigger vocabulary is also more likely to feel comfortable tackling the meaning of new words he or she finds in a reading assignment. This willingness to struggle with unfamiliar words is crucial in motivating students to keep reading.

Instruction that promotes active engagement with the vocabulary, as well as repeated exposure in many contexts, improves word learning. For example, students may spend a part of class thinking about a new concept. They may identify words with similar meanings, find words that are related to the concept, describe the concept, give examples, and identify antonyms. As they learn more, they may rethink and revise, coming to a deeper understanding. Building these meaningful associations is critical to helping students remember key concepts and vocabulary.

Teacher Reflection

What strategies do you currently use in your classroom to help students develop an in-depth understanding of specialized vocabulary?

Visual Literacy

While students must be able to read and comprehend expository text to learn social studies content, they must also interpret and analyze information from graphic features such as photos, maps, and charts. This is called visual literacy.

Teachers can help students develop visual literacy by teaching specific skills. Merely asking students to pay attention to visual aids is not enough. Engaging students in specific tasks or asking specific questions that require students to use and interact with the visuals increases the degree to which the visual improves comprehension. Three important ways to help students critically analyze visuals are to have students think about the way the visual aid was made, to have students make specific observations about details in the image, and to have students consider the photographer, chart designer, or cartographers' audience.

Literacy and Social Studies Go Hand in Hand

Providing students with instruction in higher-level reading skills and content-specific vocabulary is critical in the social studies classroom. Focusing on metacognitive strategies encourages reader independence. Specifically, students become aware of their own mental processes as they read. Familiarity with text structure allows students to formulate questions and anticipate the author's purpose. Social studies textbooks include content-specific vocabulary that requires extended instruction followed by multiple opportunities to engage with the words and develop an in-depth understanding of their meaning. Visual literacy skills must also be taught through creating tasks that use the images and thinking critically about the purpose of the image.

From Theory to Practice

Your Guide to Reading Support in myWorld Geography

my worldgeography.com

- Develop visual literary skills with Active Atlas interactive maps and Data Discovery charts and graphs.
- Make personal connections to improve comprehension through the myStory Video.
- Use the 21st Century Online Tutor to learn reading strategies.

Student Edition

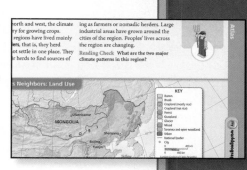

- Practice self-monitoring and check comprehension using Reading Check, Think Critically, and Section Assessment questions.
- Support content and text-structure predictions through clear headings, identification of Key Ideas, suggested reading skills, and visuals.
- Increase vocabulary using in-text and side margin definitions of Key Terms and high-frequency grade-level-appropriate vocabulary.

Student Journal

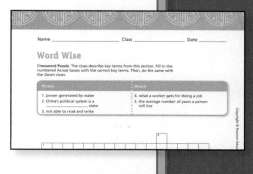

- Extend vocabulary practice with Word Wise.
- Encourage metacognition with graphic organizers in Take Notes.
- Practice text-structure identification through writing in specific genres in the Essential Question Writers Workshop.

Unit ProGuide

- Engage students in active reading and critical thinking practice with Guide on the Side questions.
- Build your own and students' background knowledge with Chapter and Section Previews and Background notes.
- Implement lesson plans with integrated reading skills instruction and practice.
- Assess reading comprehension with Section Quizzes.

Differentiated Instruction and Social Studies Content

Do your students find social studies boring? Are you teaching and reteaching core content without an improvement in student test scores? Diverse student needs, experiences, and learning styles challenge today's teachers. Many factors play a role in student achievement: learning styles, students' interests, cultural backgrounds, economic backgrounds, and social issues. Educators may improve student learning by incorporating innovative instructional strategies designed to meet students' varied needs. That is, they must personalize and differentiate instruction.

What is Differentiated Instruction?

Educators who differentiate instruction recognize students as individuals with individual learning needs. Tracking is not synonymous with differentiated instruction. While some schools group by age or reading level, differentiation implies varied approaches to learning within a heterogeneous class. Educators know that students differ in their readiness to learn, interests, experiences, and learning preferences. Teachers using differentiated instruction acknowledge these differences. They plan instruction, practice, and assessment with this student-centered, personalized instructional approach.

Why Differentiate: Two Learning Theories

By differentiating instruction, educators align teaching methods with students' learning styles. "Learning style" describes the way in which a person perceives, conceptualizes, organizes, and recalls information. Students learn more

---

Differentiated Instruction

Includes

- Challenging and engaging tasks related to the content area
- Flexible teaching techniques oriented to various learning modalities and work habits
- Opportunities for students to dem–onstrate mastery in different ways
- Integration of standards
- Use of performance assessment

Leads to

- Increased academic learning
- Improved student self-efficacy
- Enhanced motivation

efficiently when teaching methods align with how they learn. This personalized instruction motivates students and reduces the stress of learning. At the end of a differentiated lesson, more students will have met the learning objectives.

Howard Gardner's theory of Multiple Intelligences and the model of Learning Modalities address learning styles. Both offer suggestions to help students learn by using strengths and natural abilities.

Gardner's theory states that individuals have preferences and assets that affect the speed and manner in which they acquire and process information. Students' strengths influence how they understand and communicate ideas. Teachers can use these strengths as a bridge for students to cross into new and unfamiliar areas.

The Learning Modalities theory focuses on sensory modes including sight, sound, and touch. Most students learn through a combination of modalities and gain clarity of understanding when instruction engages their preferred modalities.

Learning Modalities	
Visual	process information more completely by seeing
Auditory	understand more completely when information is given verbally
Kinesthetic/ Tactile	learn best with hands-on activities, including manipulatives

Three Paths to Differentiated Instruction

Differentiating instruction requires an emotionally safe learning environment, an appropriate level of challenge for each student, and an opportunity to practice ideas and skills. Educators may differentiate in three ways:

• *Content*—the skills and knowledge students learn
• *Process*—the way in which students learn; what they do
• *Product*—how students demonstrate what they have learned

In differentiating instruction, educators can meet the diverse needs of learners while also meeting the demands of state social studies standards.

When differentiating, educators must also consider other factors that affect the learning experience. Teachers may develop lessons or group students according to psychological factors such as student interest and choice, cognitive factors such as academic achievement and skill levels, or social and motivational factors such as interpersonal skills.

Gardner's Multiple Intelligences	
Visual-Spatial	learns through seeing
Logical-Mathematical	develops concepts with numbers and linear patterns
Verbal-Linguistic	understands through language
Musical-Rhythmic	connects with rhythms, songs, and music
Bodily/ Kinesthetic	learns through tactile experiences and movement
Intrapersonal	has insights into own thinking
Interpersonal	interacts well with others
Naturalist	learns through outdoor and natural environments

Differentiating Social Studies Social studies integrates different modalities and intelligences through the varied nature of the content and skills required to interpret the content. Social studies curriculum incorporates maps, writing, recording technologies, video, online geographic applications, role-playing, field trips, and more. Futhermore, varied social studies content—from politics to art to geography—can engage learners of every learning preference.

An example from the classroom The table on the next page shows an example of how an educator might differentiate to meet a standard requiring students to analyze causes and effects of the disintegration of the Roman empire. The table shows differentiation by content, process, and product. The content varies in quantity, but not in depth of knowledge acquired. The process and product vary according to level of teacher or student control and type and modality of learning activity.

Summary

Students are distinctive in their readiness to learn, interests, and learning preferences. Students learn most effectively when educators consider ways to differentiate content, process, and product. Students learn best when they make relevant connections between curriculum, individual interests, and previous learning experiences. Core curriculum dictates what content to teach, but differentiation enables educators to diversify instruction to meet a range of learning needs. Differentiating instruction provides pathways to an accessible social studies curriculum for all students.

	Content	Process	Product
Group 1	Focus on one factor that threatened the territorial cohesion of the Roman empire.	A small teacher-directed group views a DVD about the fall of the Roman empire; teacher facilitates a discussion based on student questions.	Simulation; students record questions in journals.
Group 2	Focus on two factors that threatened the territorial cohesion of the Roman empire.	A small group, balanced between teacher-directed and student-directed, completes a "Fall of Rome" WebQuest, investigates the borders of the Roman empire at its height, and discusses the challenges of managing a vast empire.	Students make an interactive map showing the borders of the Roman empire at its height and use the map to explain the communication and military challenges of managing the empire.
Group 3	Focus on three or more factors that threatened the territorial cohesion of the Roman empire.	A small student-directed group devises a research question related to the standard, conducts research using multiple media sources, and uses a "jigsaw" to collaboratively answer the research question.	Students give a multimedia presentation describing their research question, literature reviewed, research process, and conclusions.

From Theory to Practice

Your Guide to Differentiated Instruction in myWorld Geography

my worldgeography.com

- Link to the 21st Century Online Tutor for personalized interactive instruction based on students' individual skill levels.
- Assess and respond to individual student progress with the online Self-Test.
- Provide hands-on and visual learning experiences with On Assignment.
- Assign auditory content delivery with the Online Student Edition With Audio.

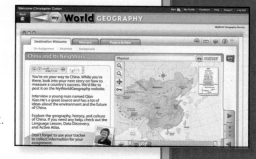

Student Edition

- Visual learners benefit from engaging photos, illustrations, maps, and charts.
- Varied content engages students with diverse personal interests.
- Students with interpersonal learning preferences enjoy myStory.
- Verbal learners gain from clear and logical text.

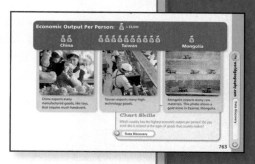

Student Journal

- Graphic organizers help visual and logical learners take notes.
- Vocabulary reinforcement provides support for linguistic learning.
- Writer's Workshop activities assist verbal processors.

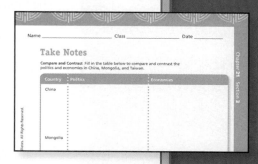

Unit ProGuide

- Text provides leveled Differentiated Instruction tips for Special Needs, Extra Support, On-Level, and Challenge throughout Section Lesson Plans and Step-by-Step Instructions.
- ELL Support boxes give suggestions for teaching students with different English-language proficiency levels.
- Background notes connect to students' varied interests.
- Hands-on activities and directions indicate Learning Styles.

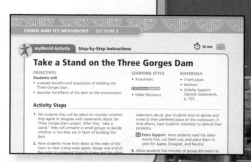

Real Learning With Activities

Good teachers know that students learn best when they tackle real-world problems that spark their curiosity and relate to their lives. Good teachers also understand their responsibility for teaching to high academic standards, helping students arrive at a deep understanding of content, and making sure students acquire the skills they will need to be successful in school and, later, at work. The challenge is to make lessons interesting and relevant for students, while making sure that real learning takes place.

Authentic Versus Active

Activity-based learning, with its emphasis on authentic products and performances, is not an educational panacea, especially when it means simply "making things." Here are some examples of activities with dubious educational value:

- To learn about state geography, 5th-grade students make state maps of clay, etch county boundaries, and paint the counties different colors.
- To learn about whales, students in a 7th-grade science class make a scale model of a sperm whale out of plastic sheeting, which they inflate with a fan.

Compare those activities with this: 8th-grade social studies students take part in a stock market competition. They research an industry (such as technology) before "buying" $1,000 worth of stock in five companies in that industry. They track the share prices and prepare a report explaining why they selected the stocks, how the stocks performed over the period, and why. They conclude by documenting what they have learned from the exercise.

One of your most important and challenging responsibilities in designing activity-based learning experiences will be to ensure that activities are high-quality, leading to real learning.

Features of High-Quality Activities

Truly high-quality activities tend to have the following characteristics:

Open-endedness—no obvious answers or solutions

Intellectual challenge and interest

In-depth exploration

Student involvement in all aspects

Special roles and tasks for tapping into students' strengths and interests

Cooperative Learning

Cooperative learning is a strategy in which small groups of students work together on common tasks. Successful activity-based learning often depends on teaching cooperative learning. Groups of students share responsibility for setting goals, assessing learning, and facilitating learning. Students question, challenge each other, discuss their ideas, and internalize learning.

According to David Johnson and Roger Johnson (1999), there are five basic elements of successful small-group learning:

- *Positive interdependence:* Students feel responsible for their own and the group's effort.
- *Face-to-face interaction:* Students encourage and support one another; the environment encourages discussion and eye contact.
- *Individual and group accountability:* Each student is responsible for doing his or her part; the group is accountable for meeting its goal.
- *Group behaviors:* Group members learn by practicing interpersonal, social, and collaborative skills.
- *Group processing:* Group members analyze their own and the group's ability to work together.

When implemented well, cooperative learning encourages achievement, active learning, discussion, confidence, and motivation. Collaboration skills such as verbalizing and justifying ideas, building consensus, disagreeing politely, and handling conflicts are increasingly valuable as more businesses organize employees into teams and task forces.

Teaching Collaborative Skills

You can help students learn the skills needed to work in groups by starting with short, structured lessons aimed at fostering taking turns, involving all students in the discussion, and clarifying the roles, rights, and responsibilities of group members. It may take time to develop a classroom community in which students respect one another, listen to one another, and feel safe enough to share their thoughts and feelings.

It is also important to establish guidelines governing how group members agree to work together. Students may not be used to working with others to complete tasks. Have groups discuss and develop guidelines that they will follow. See examples at the right.

Teachers should model positive interpersonal skills, have students practice the skills, and encourage students to reflect on how effectively they are performing the skills. After working in groups, students should engage in group-processing activities in which they discuss the interpersonal skills that influence their effectiveness in working together.

Assessing Activities

Individuals and groups must be made accountable for cooperative learning outcomes. You may choose performance assessments, group products, tests, or a combination of those things.

"Group" grades can be problematic if a few students do the majority of a group's work. An alternative is giving both a group grade for the group task and an

Examples of team guidelines:

We always treat one another with respect.

We always encourage new ideas.

We always value all suggestions.

We always justify our opinions to the team.

We always make decisions as a team.

Encouraging teamwork and 100% participation

Leading to products that demonstrate mastery of important content and skills

Application of a wide range of skills and knowledge

Clear expectations

Reliable measures of student performance

Thoughtful use of technology

Independent practice with proper scaffolding

individual grade for a subtask or specific role (see chart below). Students may also complete an individual task after the activity, such as writing a reflection about his or her learning and how the group completed the task. Individuals may also complete a final draft of a report that the group started.

Managing Class Activities

Teachers must tailor their instruction to provide remediation for students with gaps in their skills and to challenge students who have already achieved mastery. Here are some strategies to meet diverse needs.

• *Stations* are distinct areas where students work on different tasks simultaneously. Stations can be organized around ability levels so that every student can have review, challenge, and remediation. The teacher may rotate to provide instruction and assistance.

• *Compacting* allows some students to cover the curriculum in less time than the rest of the class. It assumes that students who understand a topic should not have to learn it again. While the class is covering the content, students who are compacting independently investigate the same concepts in greater depth.

• *Independent study* allows students to investigate a project independently with guidance and feedback from the teacher. Every student receives instruction at his or her own level. If a teacher notices a small group of students needs instruction in a particular skill, he or she pulls the small group aside to provide the instruction. Whole-class instruction is less frequent.

• *Leveled instruction* is when a teacher gives an introductory lesson to the entire class, then provides varying access points for students to practice skills. For example, a teacher provides several assignments with different levels of difficulty. The student or teacher chooses an assignment. Students who choose levels that seem too difficult for them tend to rise to the occasion and accomplish more.

• *Choice board assignments* are written on cards hung on a board. Students choose an assignment from a particular row or area of the board. The rows and areas are organized around specific skills.

• *Individual contracts* allow teachers to give each student a list of tasks to complete. The tasks are based on the level and ability of each student. Throughout a defined period, students work with other students who need to work on the same skill or concept. Students like the independence and choice built into the system.

Activity-based learning allows students to engage in hands-on experiences that enrich their learning and spark their intellectual curiosity. By using effective planning, grouping, and assessment strategies, teachers can ensure students acquire a deep conceptual understanding of content, and that students are able to transfer and apply knowledge.

Student Roles Within a Group

Organizer	provides the group with the overall process structure
Recorder	writes down important information (e.g., directions or group work)
Questioner	generates questions and involves all students
Assessor	evaluates the progress of each work session
Encourager	models and reinforces appropriate social skills
Spokesperson	represents the group and presents group work to rest of the class
Timekeeper	keeps the group on task and on time

From Theory to Practice

Your Guide to Activity-Based Learning in myWorld Geography

my worldgeography.com

- Have students apply knowledge from the lessons to real-world applications online.
- Make content more "active" through myWorld Videos of real young people.
- Explore the world virtually, but use data, maps, and images in real activities.

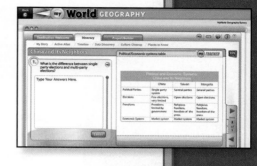

Student Edition

- Find links to myWorld Activities from related content in each section.
- Apply reading content to new situations in myWorld Activities.

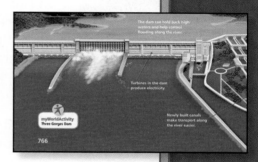

Student Journal

- Transfer information from Take Notes to relevant tasks during activities.
- Build understanding of Essential Questions to improve summative performance in myWorld Chapter Activities.

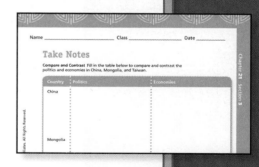

Unit ProGuide

- Support active-learning and small-group instruction with each section's myWorld Activity Step-by-Step Instructions.
- Consider More Activity Ideas that better suit your class's needs.
- Assess Enduring Understandings using the myWorld Chapter Activity and Rubric.
- Provide structure and support for myWorld Chapter Activities with each chapter's Activity Cards.

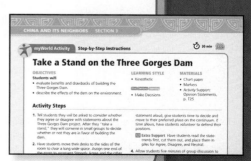

Grouping Practices Within the Social Studies Classroom

In whole-class instruction, students learn in one large group with an emphasis on uniformity of instruction. A single set of instructional objectives based on the required or core curriculum is often the focus of this grouping practice.

Classrooms are filled with great diversity. Students of varying abilities, interests, personalities, and motivations all come together within classroom walls. Social studies teachers face the task of matching the diverse needs and interests of students with the instructional objectives of the core curriculum. Teachers can use a variety of grouping practices to better meet the needs of diverse student populations. Knowing the purposes, advantages, and disadvantages of these grouping practices enables educators to make more effective instructional decisions and optimize student learning.

Whole-Class Instruction

In whole-class instruction, students learn in one large group with an emphasis on uniformity of instruction. A single set of instructional objectives based on the required or core curriculum is often the focus of this grouping practice. In this larger, whole-class setting, teacher explanation and encouragement, rather than explanation and encouragement from peers, is central to promoting student learning. Teachers may have to prepare significantly less for a whole-class lesson or activity. In addition, lessons or activities in which all students participate as a whole group expose the entire class to the same instructional objectives.

However, the emphasis on uniformity may not address the diversity of student needs and interests found in the social studies classroom. Furthermore, within a whole-class instructional setting, students may have fewer opportunities to engage with and learn from classmates.

In addition, students may be less apt to contribute to class discussion due to the size of the class and social dynamics.

Teacher Reflection

Describe specific times in your classroom when it would be beneficial to use whole-class instruction.

Which of your students appear to be at a disadvantage when you instruct in a whole-class setting? Why do you think that is?

Small-Group Instruction

Alternatively, small-group instruction occurs when students form several small groups with the emphasis on diversity of instruction and/or outcome. Small-group instruction can refer to differentiated instruction that occurs within a smaller group, or, in a broader use of the term, to the organizational structure of placing

students in small groups. We have chosen to use the term *small-group instruction* in the broader sense of the term. In simple terms, we mean grouping students in smaller numbers.

Small groups may, at times, be led by a teacher. At other times, students may work cooperatively on a clearly assigned task in a group that is small enough to allow all students to participate. Teachers may differentiate by varying instructional methods, subject matter, activities, or outcomes for each group. Alternatively, instruction may be the same for each group.

Small-group instruction facilitated by the teacher provides additional opportunities to revisit curricular content or specific skills and strategies previously taught but not yet mastered by students. Placing students in small groups for instruction can provide teachers with

more flexibility in varying the learning goals and the pace of instruction.

Productive cooperative groups emphasize peer learning and cooperation, allowing students to develop the skills of social interaction and communication. Yet, the use of small-group instruction may pose unique classroom management challenges. Diversity in instruction or tasks for various groups may require additional teacher preparation of materials. The use of small-group instruction within classrooms requires that teachers develop classroom management procedures that foster social interaction as well as the completion of specific tasks or activities.

Using small-group instruction in tandem with whole-class instruction appears to be an effective means of facilitating student learning. Yet, merely placing students into smaller teams of three to four members does not ensure that these small groupings will provide productive learning opportunities. While productivity can be defined in a variety of ways—academic achievement, conceptual learning, the use of higher-order thinking skills, engaging in high-level discourse, the occurrence of equal-status interaction, or pro-social behaviors—the nature of the tasks assigned and the types of interaction that occur within the small group need to be examined closely. In addition, it is necessary to develop protocols for small-group work to promote students' accountability within the classroom. Students must understand their individual responsibilities within the group and monitor their own progress toward the completion of assigned tasks.

Teacher Reflection:

When do you use small-group instruction in your classroom?

What are some reasons small-group instruction may not be used in the social studies classroom?

Are there activities or projects in your classroom that you could restructure to use in a small-group setting?

Group Composition

Another important consideration when using small-group instruction is group composition. Teachers may group students in many ways, ranging from common interests to similar abilities. Research on

Teacher Reflection

How would you describe a small group that is "productive"?

What are ways that teachers can encourage student accountability within small group settings?

ability-grouping practices for the past 20 years has clearly shown negative effects for some students, particularly low-achieving students and students of color. Homogenous ability groups may become stagnant, leaving little room for mobility across groups. Studies indicate that students with low ability levels learn significantly more in heterogeneous ability groups than in homogenous groups.

One response to the negative effects of homogeneous grouping for students with low ability is the use of flexible grouping practices. The purpose of flexible grouping is to group and regroup students based on specific learning needs as identified through the use of formative, or ongoing, assessment. Flexible grouping also means using a variety of grouping practices within the classroom, rather than using the same particular grouping practice for every activity.

Grouping students effectively for instruction requires consideration of the task at hand; time available for instruction; and the diverse abilities, interests, and personalities of students. Purposeful grouping allows teachers to differentiate instruction to meet student needs. The variety of personal experience and prior knowledge students bring with them to a social studies lesson provides the opportunity for students to construct meaning through diverse conversations and group projects.

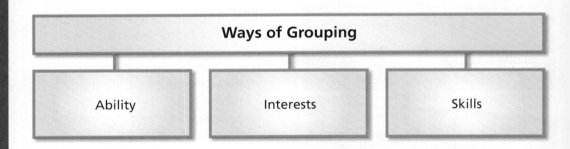

Ways of Grouping

Ability	Interests	Skills

From Theory to Practice

Your Guide to Grouping Practices in myWorld Geography

my worldgeography.com

- Have students use the Student Edition Online With Audio in small groups of mixed English-language proficiency levels
- Use On Assignment online activities during small-group instruction time
- Group students with varied interests to go On Assignment for a broader virtual exploration of a region

Student Edition

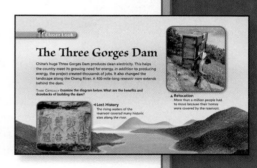

- Improve comprehension with paired reading
- Assign portions of a chapter or section to different groups who then teach that content to the class

Student Journal

- Have students collaborate on Word Wise and quiz each other on new vocabulary and Key Terms
- Conduct peer editing of Essential Question Writer's Workshop essays while you hold one-on-one or small-group writing conferences

Unit ProGuide

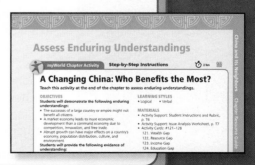

- Assign engaging learning activities for every section that implement a variety of grouping strategies
- Follow the grouping key to know which myWorld Activities work best for individuals, pairs, small groups, or the whole class
- Use Guide on the Side questions to lead whole-class guided reading

Assessing Learning in Social Studies

Assessment should focus, guide, and support instruction. Teachers should make observations about students' strengths and weaknesses, analyze performance with respect to specific goals and criteria, and constantly assemble information from a variety of sources. Assessment must be used to identify goals and strategies, monitor progress, evaluate results, and improve performance.

Types of Assessment

Assessment takes a variety of formats. Traditional assessments focus on tests or written work such as essays. Performance assessments show learning in active and nontraditional formats. Alternative assessments range from metacognitive activities, such as journals, to student-generated assessments such as portfolios.

Formative assessment Formative assessment is often informal. It happens throughout the instructional process to monitor progress and provide feedback, allowing students to correct errors and encouraging teachers to modify their methods. It helps students understand what they are doing well, links to classroom learning, and provides input to adjust the learning process. Students must use formative assessments to self-assess, evaluate their progress, and accept responsibility for managing their learning. Teachers must help students understand the importance of this process and teach methods for reflection and self-evaluation.

Summative assessment Summative assessments are used to formally gauge student learning at particular points in time. They commonly occur at the end of chapters, units, or school terms to determine what students know. They can be used to track progress and reveal areas that need review. Tests and quizzes are the most common summative assessments.

Balancing assessments Proper utilization of assessment tools in the classroom will lead to greater learning. Incorporating a variety of assessments allows for a more fully developed picture of students' learning processes. The more information teachers have about students, the better they can judge teaching quality and student learning.

Document-Based Assessment

Students read and analyze primary source documents to acquire knowledge and develop critical thinking skills. Document analysis has also become an important assessment tool. Both the Advanced Placement examinations and many state-mandated tests incorporate document-based questions. Writing tasks may ask students to think critically about sources, form opinions guided by a prompt, and present their analysis in an essay.

Teach with primary sources Students need direct instruction in using primary sources and evaluating conflicting interpretations. They also need repeated opportunities to practice these skills both in class and independently. Teach students to analyze primary and secondary sources by modeling a series of scaffolded questions that help students identify the document's purpose. Begin by asking questions with concrete answers. These will form a basis for critical thinking. Consider these questions: *What kind of document is this? Who wrote it? Why was it written? Who is the intended audience?* The purpose of these questions is to help students identify relevant information contained in the document. The questions may also spark a class discussion or act as a focus for independent practice. Ultimately, students will evaluate documents on their own.

Differentiate with documents Students may use documents to apply concepts they are learning to new situations and to extend learning beyond a textbook. Document analysis can also play an important role in differentiation. It may lead to small-group or whole-class discussion, written reports, in-class presentations, role-playing, or other instructional strategies.

Build skills with primary sources Primary source analysis increases students' critical thinking skills, prepares them for document-based questions on high-stakes tests, and reinforces the skills needed for effective citizenship. These skills include

- applying information they have learned in their study of geography.
- evaluating the reliability of sources.
- identifying the point of view of those sources and determining bias.
- identifying problems and considering a variety of solutions.

- considering issues from multiple perspectives.
- building support for a viewpoint by choosing accurate, relevant evidence.

Rubrics

A rubric is a set of guidelines for assessing student work on a continuum of quality. Holistic rubrics give an overall impression of students' work. Analytic rubrics assign separate scores for distinct criteria. Rubrics are useful when assessing reasoning, composition, and evaluation skills.

Rubrics allow students to self-assess before submitting work. A clear definition of expectations helps students to perform at the best of their ability. Students also begin to understand what areas they need to work on in order to improve.

Rubrics answer these questions:
- By what criteria will performance be judged?
- What are the elements of a quality performance?
- What does performance at each level look like?

Assessment should focus, guide, and support instruction.

Skills Developed by Studying Primary Sources

- evaluating the reliability of sources

- identifying the point of view of those sources and determining bias

- identifying problems and considering alternative solutions

- considering issues from multiple perspectives

- building support for a viewpoint by choosing accurate, relevant evidence

Designing rubrics A strong rubric

- uses descriptive language, stating what each level of quality looks like. The best rubrics thus minimize value language ("Great work," "Poor job") or mere comparisons across levels ("not as thorough as a 3") to provide the most useful feedback.
- discriminates among performance levels validly—by the key features and difference in the levels of quality, not by what is easy to count or score.
- is general enough to enable inference to broad goals and state standards, but specific enough to enable useful feedback on a particular task.
- avoids combining independent criteria in the same descriptor. For example, "accuracy of facts" and "quality of the argument" are independent traits (i.e., facts may be accurate but reasoning poor and vice versa). This factor highlights the trade-off with holistic vs. analytic scoring: holistic is easier because it throws all the criteria together in one description; analytic is more work, but provides better feedback because each trait is scored separately.
- is based on specific work samples. The rubric summarizes the traits of samples of work at each level.

Rubrics reflect different aspects of performance In a complex performance, there are several simultaneous aims with distinct traits to consider. These include

- content vs. process
- quality of understanding vs. quality of the performance
- mechanics, organization, and facts vs. the style of student writing

Rubrics must address these different aspects of performance to ensure that the evaluation is valid and that the feedback is helpful and mindful of the trade-offs of time vs. accuracy. When constructing rubrics, consider IMPACT, WORK QUALITY, PROCESS, and CONTENT as different goals.

If you are new to rubrics, you may feel most comfortable starting with one holistic rubric or a rubric focusing on a single trait. Over time you may wish to have a set of rubrics related to the four categories above that you draw from over the course of a year. Rest assured the effort is worth it. Students will better understand what you are after, and the assessment process will actually be a key element of instruction instead of just a chore.

Indicator	Description
impact of performance	refers to the success of performance, given the purposes, goals, and desired results
work quality and craftsmanship	refers to the overall polish, organization, and rigor of the work
adequacy of process/methods/behavior	refers to the quality of the procedures and manner of presentation, prior to and during performance
validity of content	refers to the correctness of the ideas, skills, or materials used

From Theory to Practice

Your Guide to Assessment in myWorld Geography

 worldgeography.com

- Have students check their learning with online self-tests.
- Assess understanding of chapter big ideas through an Essential Question-based On Assignment project.
- Diagnose and monitor student progress with SuccessTracker.

Student Edition

- Check acquisition of new knowledge with Section Assessment questions.
- Monitor progress toward understanding with Essential Question links in every Section Assessment.
- Assess chapter content, critical thinking skills, map skills, and DBQ readiness with the Chapter Assessment.

Student Journal

- Track student understanding of new vocabulary and Key Ideas with Take Notes and Word Wise.
- Evaluate students' writing progress with the Essential Question Writer's Workshop exercises in essay and paragraph forms.

Unit ProGuide

- Administer Section Quizzes to assess Key Terms and Ideas.
- Find answers to Chapter Assessment questions.
- Use Plan With Understanding by Design pages to "begin with the end in mind" and plan instruction around desired long-term results.
- Evaluate student performance in myWorld Chapter Activities with tailored rubrics.

Correlation to the National Council for the Social Studies Standards

MyWorld Geography is correlated with the knowledge standards from Expectations of Excellence, the Curriculum Standards for Social Studies. These standards were developed by the National Council for the Social Studies to address overall curriculum design.

A description of each theme is drawn from the draft standards released by the National Council for the Social Studies in October 2008. An updated version of this chart can be found at myWorldPearson.com.

THEME AND DESCRIPTION	MYWORLD GEOGRAPHY
Theme I: Culture	
Human beings create, learn, and adapt to culture. Culture helps people to understand themselves as both individuals and members of various groups. Human cultures exhibit both similarities and differences. All, for example, have systems of belief, knowledge, values, and traditions. Each is also unique. In a multicultural democratic society, students need to understand multiple perspectives that derive from different cultural vantage points. This understanding allows them to relate to people in this and other nations.	Core Concepts, Part 7 Central America and the Caribbean, Section 3 Ancient and Medieval Europe, Sections 1–5 Western Europe, Sections 1–4 Russia, Sections 1, 2 West and Central Africa, Section 3 Arabia and Iraq, Section 2 Israel and Its Neighbors, Section 2 Central Asia and the Caucasus, Section 3 South Asia, Section 2 Australia and the Pacific, myStory
Cultures are dynamic and change over time. The study of culture prepares students to ask and answer questions such as: What is culture and what roles does it play in human and societal development? What are the common characteristics of different cultures? How is unity developed within and among cultures? What is the role of diversity within society? How is diversity maintained within a culture? How do belief systems, such as religion or political ideals, influence other parts of a culture? How does culture change to accommodate different ideas and beliefs?	Essential Questions related to Theme I: • Is conflict unavoidable? • What are the challenges of diversity? • What makes a nation?

THEME AND DESCRIPTION	MYWORLD GEOGRAPHY
Theme II: Time, Continuity, and Change	
People need to understand their roots and to locate themselves in time and place. Histories and cultures integrate stories about peoples, nations, and events to help identify roots that feature both continuity as well as change over time. Understanding the theme of Time, Continuity, and Change involves actively seeking knowledge of the past and learning the ways in which people, societies, nations, and cultures retain many traditions but also change, today more rapidly than ever. Studying changes over time helps us to become grounded in knowledge about the past, enabling us to more fully understand the present and make informed decisions about the future. The appreciation for historical perspectives leads us as responsible citizens to draw on what we know about the past in shaping the future. Knowing how to read, reconstruct, and interpret the past allows us to develop a historical understanding and to answer questions such as: Why is the past important to us today? How has the world changed and how might it change in the future? How do we learn about the past? What is a reliable account of past eras and events? How can the perspective we have about our own life experiences be viewed as part of the larger human story across time? How do historical perspectives reflect varying points of view and inform contemporary ideas and actions?	Core Concepts, Part 9 All chapters, Section 2* Caribbean South America, Section 1 The Andes and the Pampas, Sections 1, 3 Brazil, myStory, Section 3 Ancient and Medieval Europe, Sections 1–4 Europe in Modern Times, Sections 1–4 Western Europe, Sections 2–4 Russia, Sections 2–3 West and Central Africa, Section 2 Southern and Eastern Africa, Section 2 South Asia, Sections 1, 3 Southeast Asia, myStory, Sections 1, 3 Essential Questions related to Theme II: • How can you measure success? • Is conflict unavoidable? • What are the challenges of diverisity?
Theme III: People, Places, and Environments	
Technological advances connect students at all levels to the world beyond their personal locations. Geography helps students understand the world they live in and gives them insight into where things are located, why they are there, and why students should care. The study of people, places, and human-environment interactions assists learners as they develop their spatial views and geographic perspectives of the world. This area of study helps learners make informed and critical decisions about the relationships between human beings and their environment. Today's social, cultural, economic, and civic demands on individuals mean that students will need the knowledge, skills, and understanding to ask and answer questions such as: How do people interact with the environment and what are some consequences of those interactions? Why is location important? What physical and human characteristics lead to the creation of regions? Why do people move and decide to live where they do? What are the implications of natural and human interaction on the environment? How do maps, globes and other geographic tools contribute to understanding of people, places, and environments?	Core Concepts, Parts 1–7 All chapters, Chapter Atlas* All chapters, Section 2* All Unit Closer activities Caribbean South America, myStory Essential Questions related to Theme III: • How much does geography shape a country? • Is it better to be independent or interdependent? • Who should benefit from a country's resources? • What makes a nation? *Does not include *Ancient and Medieval Europe* and *Early Modern Europe*

THEME AND DESCRIPTION	MYWORLD GEOGRAPHY
Theme IV: Individual Development and Identity	
Personal identity is shaped by one's culture, by groups, and by institutional influences. Given the nature of individual development in one's own cultural context, students need to be aware of the processes of learning, growth, and development at every level of their own school experiences. Examination of various forms of human behavior enhances understanding of the relationships among social norms and emerging personal identities, the social processes that influence identity formation, and the ethical principles underlying individual action. Questions around identity and development are central to the understanding of who we are. Such questions include: How do individuals grow and change physically, emotionally, and intellectually? Why do individuals behave as they do? What influences how people learn, perceive, and grow? How do people meet their basic needs in a variety of contexts? How do individuals develop over time?	All chapters, myStory Caribbean South America, Section 3 The Andes and the Pampas, Section 2 Essential Questions related to Theme IV: • What are the challenges of diversity? • How can you measure success? • Is it better to be independent or interdependent?
Theme V: Individuals, Groups, and Institutions	
Institutions are the formal and informal political, economic, and social organizations that help us carry out, organize, and manage our daily affairs. They also help mediate conflicts. Institutions such as schools, churches, families, government agencies, and the courts all play an integral role in our lives. These and other institutions exert enormous influence over us, yet institutions are no more than organizational embodiments to further the core social values of those who comprise them. It is important that students know how institutions are formed, what controls and influences them, how they control and influence individuals and culture, and how institutions can be maintained or changed. The study of individuals, groups, and institutions, drawing upon sociology, anthropology, and other disciplines, prepares students to ask and answer questions such as: What is the role of institutions in this and other societies? How am I influenced by institutions? How do institutions change? What is my role in institutional change?	Core Concepts, Part 7, Lesson 2 Core Concepts, Part 8, Lessons 3, 4 Ancient and Medieval Europe, Sections 1–4 Europe in Modern Times, Sections 1, 3–5 Western Europe, Section 2–4 West and Central Africa, Section 3 Russia, Sections 2–3 Essential Questions related to Theme V: • What should governments do? • Is it better to be independent or interdependent? • Who should benefit from a country's resources?

THEME AND DESCRIPTION	MYWORLD GEOGRAPHY
Theme VI: Power, Authority, and Governance	
Understanding the foundations of political thought, the historical development of various structures of power, authority, and governance and their evolving functions in contemporary U.S. society, as well as in other parts of the world, is essential for developing civic competence. By examining the purposes and characteristics of various governance systems, learners develop an understanding of how groups and nations attempt to resolve conflicts and seek to establish order and security. In exploring this theme, students confront questions such as: What are the purposes and functions of government? Under what circumstances is the exercise of political power legitimate? What are the proper scope and limits of authority? How are individual rights protected within the context of majority rule? What conflicts exist among fundamental principles and values of constitutional democracy? What are the rights and responsibilities of citizens in a constitutional democracy?	Core Concepts, Part 8, Lessons 2–5 United States, Section 2 Ancient and Medieval Europe, Sections 1–4 Europe in Modern Times, Sections 1–5 Western Europe, Sections 2–4 Russia, Sections 2, 3 Southern and Eastern Africa, Section 3 The Andes and the Pampas, Sections 2, 3 Japan and the Koreas, Section 3 Australia and the Pacific, Section 3 Essential Questions related to Theme VI: • What should governments do? • Is conflict unavoidable? • What makes a nation?
Theme VII: Production, Distribution, and Consumption	
People have wants that often exceed the limited resources available to them. Unequal distribution of resources necessitates systems of exchange, including trade, to improve the well-being of the economy, while the role of government in economic policymaking varies over time and from place to place. Increasingly these decisions are global in scope and require systematic study of an interdependent world economy and the role of technology in economic decision making. As a result, a variety of ways have been invented to decide upon answers to four fundamental questions: What is to be produced? How is production to be organized? How are goods and services to be distributed? In exploring this theme, students confront such questions as: What factors influence decision making around issues of the production, distribution, and consumption of goods? What is the most effective allocation of the factors of production (land, labor, capital, and management)? What are the best ways to deal with market failures? How does interdependence brought on by globalization impact local social systems?	Core Concepts, Part 5, Lessons 1–6 United States, Section 3 Caribbean and Central America, Section 3 Brazil, Section 3 Ancient and Medieval Europe, Sections 1–4 Western Europe, Sections 2–4 North Africa, Section 3 China and Its Neighbors, Sections 2, 3 Essential Questions related to Theme VII: • Is it better to be independent or interdependent? • Who should benefit from a country's resources? • Is conflict unavoidable?

THEME AND DESCRIPTION	MYWORLD GEOGRAPHY
Theme VIII: Science, Technology, and Society	
Science and its application, technology, affect cultural change and people's interaction with their world. Technological advances allow people around the world to be connected instantaneously beyond their immediate locations. Modern life as we know it would be impossible without technology and the science that supports it. But both raise many questions about how we perceive our culture and the role science and technology play in our lives. Is new technology always better than that which it will replace? What can we learn from the past about how new technologies result in broader social change, some of which is unanticipated? How can we cope with the ever-increasing pace of change, perhaps even with the feeling that technology has gotten out of control? How can we manage technology so that the greatest numbers of people benefit? How can we preserve our fundamental values and beliefs in a world that is rapidly becoming one technology-linked village? How do science and technology affect our sense of self and morality? How are disparate cultures, geographically separated, impacted by events, e.g., the spread of AIDS?	Core Concepts, Part 7, Lesson 7 Caribbean South America, Section 3 The Andes and the Pampas, Section 3 Ancient and Medieval Europe, Sections 1, 2, 4 Europe in Modern Times, Sections 1–3, 5 Western Europe, Sections 2–4 Russia, Sections 2,3 Arabia and Iraq, Section 3 South Asia, Sections 1, 3 Southeast Asia, myStory, Section 3 Essential Questions related to Theme VIII: • How can you measure success? • Is conflict unavoidable? • Is it better to be independent or interdependent?
Theme IX: Global Connections	
Globalization has intensified and accelerated the changes faced at the local, national, and international level. The effects are evident in the rapidly changing social, economic, and political institutions and systems. Technology has removed or lowered many barriers bringing far-flung cultures together. The connections we have to the rest of the world provide opportunities for creativity and empowerment, yet they also create power vacuums that bring about uncertainty. The realities of global interdependence require understanding the increasingly important and diverse global connections among world societies. In exploring this theme, students confront questions such as: What is "globalization" and what are its consequences? What are the benefits from and problems associated with global interdependence? How should people and societies balance global connectedness with the need for local roots? What is needed for life to thrive on an ever-changing, shrinking planet?	Central America and the Caribbean, Section 3 Caribbean South America, Section 3 Brazil, Sections 2, 3 Russia, Section 3 Southern and Eastern Africa, Section 3 Iran, Turkey, and Cyprus, Section 3 Central Asia and the Caucasus, Section 2 Essential Questions related to Theme IX: • What makes a nation? • Is conflict unavoidable? • Who should benefit from a country's resources? • Is it better to be independent or interdependent?

THEME AND DESCRIPTION	MYWORLD GEOGRAPHY
Theme X: Civic Ideals and Practices	
An understanding of civic ideals and practices of citizenship is critical to full participation in society and is a central purpose of the social studies. All people have a stake in examining civic ideals and practices across time and in diverse societies as well as at home, and in determining how to close the gap between present practices and the ideals upon which our democratic republic is based. Questions faced by students studying this might be: What is the balance between rights and responsibilities? What is civic participation? How do citizens become involved? What is the role of the citizen in the community and the nation, and as a member of the world community?	Core Concepts, Part 8, Lesson 5 Ancient and Medieval Europe, Sections 1, 2 Europe in Modern Times, Sections 1, 3–5 Western Europe, Sections 2–4 Russia, Sections 2, 3 Central Asia and the Caucasus, Section 3 Essential Questions related to Theme X: • What makes a nation? • What should governments do? • What are the challenges of diversity?

TEACHER TIP

The NCSS Expectations of Excellence are curriculum standards rather than content standards. Using the Expectations of Excellence, your state standards, and the resources available to you through the *myWorld* program, you can create a curriculum that best meets the needs of your students.

Correlation to Geography for Life, the National Geography Standards

MyWorld Geography is correlated with Geography for Life, the National Geography Standards. These standards were prepared by the Geography Education Project, a partnership of the American Geographical Society, the Association of American Geographers, the National Council for Geographic Education, and the National Geographic Society. Concepts and skills contained in the Geography Standards are incorporated throughout the program. This correlation displays places where the Standards are directly addressed.

STANDARD	MYWORLD GEOGRAPHY
The World in Spatial Terms	
Standard 1 Use maps and other geographic representations, tools, and technologies to acquire, process, and report information from a spatial perspective.	Core Concepts, Part 1 Core Concepts, Part 9, Section 4 All chapters, Chapter Atlas
Standard 2 Use mental maps to organize information about people, places, and environments in a spatial context.	All chapters, Chapter Atlas All chapters, Chapter Assessment
Standard 3 Analyze the spatial organization of people, places, and environments on Earth's surface.	All chapters, Chapter Atlas
Places and Regions	
Standard 4 Understand the physical and human characteristics of places.	All chapters, Chapter Atlas
Standard 5 Understand that people create regions to interpret Earth's complexity.	Core Concepts, Part 1, Section 2
Standard 6 Understand how culture and experience influence people's perception of places and regions.	Core Concepts, Part 1, Section 1 Israel and Its Neighbors, Section 3 Iran, Turkey, and Cyprus, Section 3
Physical Systems	
Standard 7 Understand the physical processes that shape the patterns of Earth's surface.	Core Concepts, Part 2 Core Concepts, Part 4 Caribbean and Central America, Section 1 Western Europe, Section 1
Standard 8 Understand the characteristics and spatial distribution of ecosystems on Earth's surface.	Core Concepts, Part 3, Section 6 Mexico, Section 1 Brazil, Section 1 Southern and Eastern Africa, Section 1

STANDARD	MYWORLD GEOGRAPHY
Human Systems	
Standard 9 Understand the characteristics, distribution, and migration of human populations on Earth's surface.	Core Concepts, Part 6, Section 3 All chapters, Chapter Atlas
Standard 10 Understand the characteristics, distribution, and complexity of Earth's cultural mosaics.	Core Concepts, Part 7, Section 7 The Andes and the Pampas, Section 3 Iran, Turkey, and Cyprus, Section 3 Southeast Asia, Section 3
Standard 11 Understand the patterns and networks of economic interdependence on Earth's surface.	Caribbean and Central America, Section 3 Western Europe, Section 3 Core Concepts, Part 5 Mexico, Section 3
Standard 12 Understand the processes, patterns, and functions of human settlement.	Core Concepts, Part 6 North Africa, Section 1 South Asia, Section 1
Standard 13 Understand how the forces of cooperation and conflict among people influence division and control of Earth's surface.	Canada, Section 2 Caribbean South America, Section 2 Southern and Eastern Africa, Section 2 Israel and Its Neighbors, Section 2
Environment and Society	
Standard 14 Understand how human actions modify the physical environment.	Core Concepts, Part 4 Caribbean and Central America, Section 1 Brazil, Section 3 Eastern Europe, Section 1 North Africa, Section 1
Standard 15 Understand how physical systems affect human systems.	Core Concepts, Part 4 Mexico, Section 1 North Africa, Section 1 Arabia and Iraq, Section 1 Japan and the Koreas, Section 1 Canada, Section 1
Standard 16 Understand the changes that occur in the meaning, use, distribution, and importance of resources.	Brazil, Section 3 West and Central Africa, Sections 1 and 2 Russia, Section 1 Arabia and Iraq, Sections 1 and 2 Central Asia and the Caucasus, Section 1
The Uses of Geography	
Standard 17 Understand how to apply geography to interpret the past.	Ancient and Medieval Europe, Sections 1–4 Europe in Modern Times, Sections 1–4 South Asia, Section 1
Standard 18 Understand how to apply geography to interpret the present and plan for the future.	All chapters, Section 3

myWorld Geography Pacing Guide

Pearson's *myWorld Geography* offers a flexible, integrated approach to teaching geography. You will choose from an innovative menu of instructional strategies to build a curriculum and learning experiences that best meet your students' needs and your state's content requirements. Using your state standards as a guide, choose the sections, activities, and Core Concepts lessons that meet your teaching needs. Use the Lesson Planner at the end of this book to record the strategies you will use in class.

Sections may be covered in one or two class periods. A one-day option may include guided reading in class or, if students read for homework, a myWorld Activity. A two-day option includes one day for guided reading and one day for the activity.

Core Concepts focus on the foundations of geography that students must understand to access content across all chapters. Each concept is divided into lessons that may be taught at the beginning of the school year or integrated into chapter and section lessons.

Sample chapter: Central America and the Caribbean

Section & Time	Option 1 (Students read on their own.)	Option 2 (Students read in class.)
Introduction 30 minutes	Connect to the Essential Question: Is it better to be independent or interdependent?	Read myStory and view myStory video; complete *Working for the Future* in the Student Journal.
Section 1: Chapter Atlas 40-45 minutes	1. Choose a Connect activity Core Concepts: Climate and Weather 2. Experience myWorld Activity: Location Equation (20 min) 3. Understand	1. Choose a Connect activity 2. Experience Read in class, modeling active reading with the Guide on the Side and have students take notes in the Student Journal. 3. Understand
Section 2: History of Central America and the Caribbean 40-45 minutes	1. Choose a Connect activity 2. Experience Complete an Active Atlas activity in the Student Center and the myWorld Activity: Corners of History 3. Understand	1. Choose a Connect activity 2. Experience Read in class, modeling active reading with the Guide on the Side and have students complete an activity from the 21st Century Learning Online Tutor and apply the skill. 3. Understand
Section 3: Central America and the Caribbean Today 40-45 minutes	1. Choose a Connect activity 2. Experience Core Concepts: Economic Development myWorld Activity: Is Free Fair? (30 min) 3. Understand	1. Choose a Connect activity 2. Experience Read in class, modeling active reading with the Guide on the Side and have students take notes in the Student Journal. 3. Understand
Chapter Assessment Times will vary.	Chapter Activity: Venturing in Nicaragua, Chapter Test, or On Assignment Presentation	Essential Question essay in Student Journal, Chapter Assessment questions in text, or Section Quiz

Lesson or Activity	Minutes
Core Concepts	
Part 1: Tools of Geography (5 lessons)	100
Part 2: Our Planet, Earth (5 lessons)	100
Part 3: Climates and Ecosystems (6 lessons)	120
Part 4: Human–Environment Interaction (3 lessons)	60
Part 5 : Economics and Geography (6 lessons)	120
Part 6: Population and Movement (4 lessons)	80
Part 7: Culture and Geography (7 lessons)	140
Part 8: Government and Citizenship (5 lessons)	100
Part 9: Tools of History (4 lessons)	80
United States and Canada	
Regional Overview	15
The United States	
myStory: Finding Opportunity	20–45
Chapter Atlas	45–90
History of the United States	45–90
The United States Today	45–90
Case Study: The United States Expands	20–45
Primary Source: American Democracy	20–45
Chapter Activity: Interviewing America	120
Chapter Assessment	45
Canada	
myStory: Drawing on Heritage	20–45
Chapter Atlas	45–90
History of Canada	45–90
Canada Today	45–90
Case Study: Canada's Icy North	20–45
Primary Source: Defining Canada	20–45
Chapter Activity: Moving to Canada	90
Chapter Assessment	45
Unit Closer Activity: Work in Teams	45–60

Lesson or Activity	Minutes
Middle America	
Regional Overview	15
Mexico	
myStory: A Long Way From Home	20–45
Chapter Atlas	45–90
History of Mexico	45–90
Mexico Today	45–90
Case Study: Rise and Fall of the Aztecs	20–45
Primary Source: The Mexican Revolution	20–45
Chapter Activity: A Time for Judgment	60
Chapter Assessment	45
Central America and the Caribbean	
myStory: Working for the Future	20–45
Chapter Atlas	45–90
History of Central America and the Caribbean	45–90
Central America and the Caribbean Today	45–90
Case Study: Cuba: Revolution to Today	20–45
Primary Source: The Maya	20–45
Chapter Activity: Venturing in Nicaragua	120
Chapter Assessment	45
Unit Closer Activity: Solve Problems	45–60

TEACHER TIP

MyWorld Geography lessons were built using the Understanding by Design model. A consistent focus on essential questions and enduring understandings helps students make connections between different times and places. Learn how to implement Understanding by Design by reading Grant Wiggins' essay on page 16.

Lesson or Activity	Minutes
South America	
Regional Overview	15
Caribbean South America	
myStory: Daniella's Coffee Run	20–45
Chapter Atlas	45–90
History of Caribbean South America	45–90
Caribbean South America Today	45–90
Case Study: Civil Conflict in Colombia	20–45
Primary Source: Union or Separation?	20–45
Chapter Activity: Hunt for Resources	120
Chapter Assessment	45
The Andes and the Pampas	
myStory: Under the Rich Mountain	20–45
Chapter Atlas	45–90
History of the Andes and the Pampas	45–90
The Andes and the Pampas Today	45–90
Case Study: Bolivia: A Divided Nation	20–45
Primary Source: The Incas	20–45
Chapter Activity: Grant Report	120
Chapter Assessment	45
Brazil	
myStory: Vinicius's Game Plan	20–45
Chapter Atlas	45–90
History of Brazil	45–90
Brazil Today	45–90
Case Study: Destruction of the Amazon Rain Forest	20–45
Primary Source: Describing Brazil's Landscape	20–45
Chapter Activity: Job Hunting in Brazil	120
Chapter Assessment	45
Unit Closer Activity: Search for Information on the Internet	45–60

Lesson or Activity	Minutes
Europe and Russia	
Regional Overview	15
Ancient and Medieval Europe	
myStory: A Prophecy Fulfilled	20–45
Ancient Greece	45–90
Ancient Rome	45–90
Early Middle Ages	45–90
High and Late Middle Ages	45–90
Primary Source: Ancient Greek Literature	20–45
Primary Source: The Fall of the Roman Empire	20–45
Primary Source: Learned Women of the Middle Ages	20–45
Chapter Activity: Piecing Together the Past	120
Chapter Assessment	45
Europe in Modern Times	
myStory: The Battle of the Spanish Armada	20–45
New Ways of Thinking	45–90
Europe Expands	45–90
An Age of Revolutions	45–90
Wars and Hardship	45–90
Rebuilding and New Challenges	45–90
Primary Source: Renaissance Views of Rulers	20–45
Primary Source: Democracy in Eastern Europe	20–45
Primary Source: The World Wars in Art	20–45
Chapter Activity: Technology: Then and Now	120
Chapter Assessment	45

Lesson or Activity	Minutes
Europe and Russia (continued)	
Western Europe	
myStory: Europe at Her Doorstep	20–45
Chapter Atlas	45–90
Northwestern Europe Today	45–90
West Central Europe Today	45–90
Southern Europe Today	45–90
Case Study: Energy for the Future	20–45
Primary Source: A Sense of Identity	20–45
Chapter Activity: Norway and the European Union	120
Chapter Assessment	45
Eastern Europe	
myStory: Serhiy's Leap	20–45
Chapter Atlas	45–90
Eastern Europe Today	45–90
Case Study: Influence of Religion on Cultures of Eastern Europe	20–45
Primary Source: Ethnic Conflict in Bosnia	20–45
Chapter Activity: Open for Business	120
Chapter Assessment	45
Russia	
myStory: Boris's Bigspin	20–45
Chapter Atlas	45–90
History of Russia	45–90
Russia Today	45–90
Case Study: The Soviet Industrial Legacy	20–45
Primary Source: The Russian Revolution	20–45
Chapter Activity: Memo to Russia	120
Chapter Assessment	45
Unit Closer Activity: Analyze Media Content	45–60

Lesson or Activity	Minutes
Africa	
Regional Overview	15
West and Central Africa	
myStory: A String of Dreams	20–45
Chapter Atlas	45–90
History of West and Central Africa	45–90
West and Central Africa Today	45–90
Case Study: Famous Cities and Kingdoms of West Africa	20–45
Primary Source: Things Fall Apart	20–45
Chapter Activity: To Drill or Not to Drill?	60
Chapter Assessment	45
Southern and Eastern Africa	
myStory: A Hopeful Song	20–45
Chapter Atlas	45–90
History of Southern and Eastern Africa	45–90
Southern and Eastern Africa Today	45–90
Case Study: The Impact of Colonialism	20–45
Primary Source: Literature of Southern and Eastern Africa	20–45
Chapter Activity: Agents of Change	90
Chapter Assessment	45
North Africa	
myStory: Shaimaa's Neighborhood	20–45
Chapter Atlas	45–90
History of North Africa	45–90
North Africa Today	45–90
Case Study: Ancient Egyptian Culture	20–45
Primary Source: Reform in Morocco	20–45
Chapter Activity: National Crest Contest	90
Chapter Assessment	45
Unit Closer Activity: Generate New Ideas	45–60

Lesson or Activity	Minutes
Southwest Asia	
Regional Overview	15
Arabia and Iraq	
myStory: Hanan's Call to Care	20–45
Chapter Atlas	45–90
History of Arabia and Iraq	45–90
Arabia and Iraq Today	45–90
Case Study : Patterns of Government in Arabia and Iraq	20–45
Primary Source: The Roles of Men and Women in Islam	20–45
Chapter Activity: Water for Arabia and Iraq	120
Chapter Assessment	45
Israel and Its Neighbors	
myStory: Maayan and Muhammad	20–45
Chapter Atlas	45–90
History of Israel and Its Neighbors	45–90
Israel and Its Neighbors Today	45–90
Case Study: Religious Traditions and Art	20–45
Primary Source: Voices of Fear and Hope	20–45
Chapter Activity: History Museum Tour	90
Chapter Assessment	45
Iran, Turkey, and Cyprus	
myStory: Bilal Looks Forward	20–45
Chapter Atlas	45–90
History of Iran, Turkey, and Cyprus	45–90
Iran, Turkey, and Cyprus Today	45–90
Case Study: The Kurdish People	20–45
Primary Source: The Iranian Revolution	20–45
Chapter Activity: Regional Ethnic Cooperation Conference	120
Chapter Assessment	45
Unit Closer Activity: Make a Difference	45–60

Lesson or Activity	Minutes
South and Central Asia	
Regional Overview	15
Central Asia and the Caucasus	
myStory: Askar Serves His People	20–45
Chapter Atlas	45–90
History of Central Asia and the Caucasus	45–90
Central Asia and the Caucasus Today	45–90
Case Study: Education: Reforming the Soviet System	20–45
Primary Source: Samarqand: A Silk Road City	20–45
Chapter Activity: Money Well Spent	120
Chapter Assessment	45
South Asia	
myStory: Nancy's Fruitful Loan	20–45
Chapter Atlas	45–90
History of South Asia	45–90
South Asia Today	45–90
Case Study: Governments and Citizens in South Asia	20–45
Primary Source: Nonviolent Protest	20–45
Chapter Activity: One Small Step	120
Chapter Assessment	45
Unit Closer Activity: Evaluate Web Sites	45–60

TEACHER TIP

You will notice that the *myWorld Geography* Unit ProGuides take the place of a Teacher's Edition. Each section begins with a detailed lesson plan, followed by an overview resource guide and a worksheet supporting a myWorld Activity. The "wrap" around the student pages is designed to help you teach reading skills and bolster your own knowledge of the topic discussed on the page.

Lesson or Activity	Minutes
East and Southeast Asia	
Regional Overview	15
China and Its Neighbors	
myStory: Xiao's Lake	20–45
Chapter Atlas	45–90
History of China and Its Neighbors	45–90
China and Its Neighbors Today	45–90
Case Study: Information Control: Changes in the Chinese Communist Party	20–45
Primary Source: Confucianism and Imperial Law	20–45
Chapter Activity: A Changing China: Who Benefits the Most?	120
Chapter Assessment	45
Japan and the Koreas	
myStory: Asuka: A Girl on the Go	20–45
Chapter Atlas	45–90
History of Japan and the Koreas	45–90
Japan and the Koreas Today	45–90
Case Study: Government and Citizens in Japan and the Koreas	20–45
Primary Source: Japan's Occupation of Korea	20–45
Chapter Activity: Mission Earth	120
Chapter Assessment	45
Southeast Asia	
myStory: A Minangkabau Wedding	20–45
Chapter Atlas	45–90
History of Southeast Asia	45–90
Southeast Asia Today	45–90
Case Study: Geography of a Disaster	20–45
Primary Source: Southeast Asia in the 1200s	20–45
Chapter Activity: Gaining Wealth Through History	120
Chapter Assessment	45
Unit Closer Activity: Give an Effective Presentation	45–60

Lesson or Activity	Minutes
Australia and the Pacific	
Regional Overview	15
Australia and the Pacific	
myStory: Jack Connects to His Culture	20–45
Chapter Atlas	45–90
History of Australia and the Pacific	45–90
Australia and the Pacific Today	45–90
Antarctica	45–90
Case Study: The Economy of the Pacific Islands	20–45
Primary Source: Aborigines Under British Rule	20–45
Chapter Activity: Reporting Back: A Voyage to the Pacific	120
Chapter Assessment	45
Unit Closer Activity: Develop Cultural Awareness	45–60

TEACHER TIP

Plan backward using the *myWorld Geography* Unit ProGuides. Using the objectives, Essential Questions, and your state standards as a guide, choose the learning activities that best meet your students' needs. The Unit ProGuides provide a wide variety of suggested activities to address reading and writing skills, 21st Century Learning, enrichment, students with special needs, and varied learning styles.

Day/ Class _____   Chapter/ Section _____

Essential Question _____

Enduring Understandings/ Objectives _____
_____
_____
_____

		ACTIVITY	MATERIALS/PREP
CONNECT	TIME: _____		
EXPERIENCE	TIME: _____		
UNDERSTAND	TIME: _____		